Thank you Shǎry for being a blessing to many.

In the
Hopeland

Even a Genocide Can Bring Life Back

MUKAYIRANGA EUGENIE

Gift from the author Eugénie β

Edmonton
Feb. 27- 2019

◆ FriesenPress

Suite 300 - 990 Fort St
Victoria, BC, V8V 3K2
Canada

www.friesenpress.com

Copyright © 2017 by Mukayiranga Eugenie
First Edition — 2017

Author Photo Copyrighted to Calgary Photo Studio
All pictures in this book are used with permission.

ISBN
978-1-4602-5758-6 (Hardcover)
978-1-4602-5759-3 (Paperback)
978-1-4602-5760-9 (eBook)

1. BIOGRAPHY & AUTOBIOGRAPHY, RELIGIOUS

Distributed to the trade by The Ingram Book Company

Preface

The world needs encouragers.

In 2001, I was given a vision from God to bring out to the world. I saw people dead, condemned to live in hell because of their sins. When I woke up, I wanted to shout aloud and tell the whole world about what I saw. Not being able to do so was killing me. I had to be strong and it took a lot of strength for me to trust God that one day, I would be able to. Today, I am glad to do so through this book. I deeply thank God for that.

Before writing this book, I shared my message by talking to individuals, then to groups of people, then to churches. But inside, I knew that was not enough for the story to get as far as I wanted it to go.

In 2006, one of my pastors, Pastor Nyandwi Enock, encouraged me through a phone call to write a book about the vision I was given. At the time, I was going through too much hardship that I did not have enough energy to write a book. I believe my pastor's prayers led me to meet Shari Scott, a dear friend of mine, so that the job of God would be accomplished.

What happened between Shari and me was unusual. For ten years, I had no energy to write my story until I met this wonderful Christian woman, full of love and discernment. We first met on one summer morning in 2012. I was new to Calgary and we happened to both be attending the same church: the Airdrie Campus of Centre Street Church. It was there that I told her my story. Then, in the middle of it, she stopped me and said: "Eugenie, you need to find a time to put the whole story on paper." She was always smiling and cheerful but regarding this matter, she turned into the most serious person I've ever seen. It was then that I understood how strong her message was. A message from a loving heart is almost always well received. The way she looked at me that day, it was like she was telling me "Eugenie, you are able. Hurry up, please". I slowly obeyed and started the writing process. Shari and I have been very good friends ever since. May she find my gratitude through the pages of this book. The world needs more of such an encourager.

Farther in this book, I am reminiscing, picturing my connection with Shari Scott.

How many dead people come back to life?

Among the living, only very few die and then come back to live. From those who get life back, some get understanding about why death puked them or to say it more politely, threw them up. The wise among them use their second chance to get more prepared and to prepare others before death comes back to take them for real. *That is what I am trying to do.*

I had an out-of-body experience twice. It was not only precious to me but it also came with a must-tell-mission that compels me to get out and make sure the story goes as far as possible. It was a transforming experience for me. I would like to see the same change happen in people who will hear the story, as if they themselves went through the same experience.

I want to use my second chance at life to share how I was able to get ready for death by getting ready for eternal life with God.

Before my out-of-body experience, I could do tomorrow what I should have done or said today. Today, aware of how unpredictable death is, I do not take my days for granted. I do my best to say or do what I am supposed to, taking any opportunity given to me as a possible last one. What I saw after death helps me daily to remain peaceful in times of storm, knowing more than ever before that God is coaching all that is happening to us on a 24/7 basis. I remember the speed of angels sent from heaven to be my caregivers; that increased my faith in God a thousand times! God is the closest, most powerful Being to each one of us and nothing can change my mind about that truth. This knowledge helps me to talk to him any time and any day in prayer and thanksgiving. His caring and loving presence is always there, wherever I am. Knowing that builds up my fearless attitude in whatever I do.

Can we really see angels? Do they know the Bible?

From a very young age, I believed in the Bible and the judgement of God for the good or the bad we do before we die.

I read about the angels in the Bible. I also heard some people's stories about them. Then I got a chance to see those beings through the vision I got from heaven. I got a chance to see them for real! With my very own eyes.

I knew also that the Bible is the Book of Life. Then I saw, twice, a very big Bible in the hands of an angel, telling me where to go after my death! Somewhere beyond this planet earth!

My conscience was intact, it could not die. From that time, more than ever before, I decided to do my best, with God's help, to keep my conscience clean in order to remain connected to God's mind.

I knew the meaning of the word "eternity". Then I died. All of a sudden I faced "eternity" for real: I could see it and touch it. I realized that our earthly body could not allow us to grasp the meaning of the spiritual realm as it is conceived from God's mind. I understood then why we can approach God only by faith. Hebrew 11: 6 became so true to me ever since: "People who come to God must believe that He exists and He rewards those who earnestly seek Him".

From that time on, I cherished the Book of Life more than ever before. Would you do the same? Please? I beg you, with tears deep in my soul. Discover God's invitation for Eternal joyful life in our heavenly houses now. Jesus said in John 14:2: "In my Father's house are many mansions: if it were not so, I would have told you. I go to prepare a place for you" (KJV).

I saw how angels from God are sent instantly as soon as you need help from God.

The angels I saw were obeying God for every decision He was making on my behalf. If the angels serve us upon God's command once we die, how much more do they obey Him while we are still alive? They are very busy serving us but our earthly eyes cannot catch their presence among the living. Reading my story will increase the faith of many Christians who may be in doubt about their choice in following the Bible's teaching. I saw also how the Holy Spirit in us is in permanent connection with God the Father and Jesus. They are really "Three in One", well united in a perfect harmonious coordination of what is happening here on earth.

Are you passionate for a successful life?

A person passionate for a well-achieved plan in life should make it count for ever and ever. That is the invitation from God for human kind.

I was born passionate. I work toward great goals. I believe in small steps when they lead toward the goal. When I decided to be a friend of God, I realized that He was and is a faithful partner, who never breaks His promises and who is always beside me in all that I go through every second, minute, hour, day, all lifelong. That is why I became passionate in working for God. He always puts Himself between me and opposing forces, in such a way that progress is assured already when I am at His service.

By reading this book, you will see that one of the reasons I wrote it was to share my travel underground and beyond the sky, a journey that taught me a lot about the power of God over our souls once we die. I would like people who read my story to realize that our body is the best office through which God, our creator, can deliver us from the power of death. Our body is meant to bring real life into our being and to so many people around us, if only we understood the eternal purpose of God behind each human life that he created.

People who are passionate about achieving great and ultimate goal in their life, God has them in mind. He is pleased with those who take high risk in helping others to have a better life. He is backing up all people who do good to themselves and to others.

It would be a waste of time to not fully go toward eternal perfect life in heaven. That is why I find that helping people to run away from sin and to become friends of God is the most excellent job a man can achieve. Imagine a job that God is always backing up to make it fulfilled. Turning lives toward his will is the one.

My story is one of many other invitations preparing people to be always ready to obey the God of the Bible in order to spend a happy eternity with Him once we die. This is a matter of choice between life and death now. Tomorrow may be too late dear friend, reader of this book. I saw hell: the destination of thousands of people who did not care about the Bible. I wish for no one to go there.

I hope my story may challenge those who do not believe in God or in the Bible. That they may change their mind and start to see God's work wherever they go. That they may also get inspired and discover that they have more value than what they think: knowing that all mankind are eternal beings. That pure truth gave me peace and purpose in life. Refusing the truth will not stop it from being real. Making choices is a matter of life or death for you and me. My story wants to invite people to make the best choice ever: live happy forever and ever by following Jesus' call through the Bible. The out of body experience confirmed that no one will escape the Judgment by the Bible.

What happened to me can happen to anyone. Great things happen to all people who seek God's will with a sincere and humble heart.

Book dedication

To the Scripture Union in Rwanda, through whom I dedicated my life to Christ 40 years ago.

|To those who went in Heaven before us and those, from all nations, who have a deep and sincere desire to live with God for Eternity in Heaven.

To those who help people to become true followers of Jesus Christ, especially the persecuted church of Christ, wherever they are.

To those who carry deep wounds in their souls for the truth. God knows you. He is proud of you. He knows that there are more and more wounded souls in the selfish world we live in today. He keeps loving them. He keeps calling them for true repentance. Never give up. The best is ahead.

> I dedicate this book to the Eternal King, God in heaven and among us. Only He knows why I had to face so many oppositions to see this story get out, after fifteen years of trying.

Table of Contents

Where is God? The truth is where God is and God is where the truth is. For me, the truth is God's dwelling place.

Acknowledgements

Thanks to all the people who helped me to follow Jesus and enjoy Christian life. Thanks to Pastor Gemima Mukankusi who carried me in prayers during my dark moments preparing this book. May God remember all the many hours she spent calling me from England and encouraging me to keep going no matter how hard and long the journey was!

Thanks to various people and churches who contributed to the outcome of this book. Thank you for your trust, for your prayers and **support**, especially during my hardest moments of my ministry. My sincere gratitude to pastor Wilfred Rusibira with Abasaruzi Missionary Church in Toronto and the whole congregation of EMCC. I am glad to be part of the family of faith in Jesus Christ, passionate in making disciples who make more disciples for him.

Thanks to Friesen Press Publishing Team for their help and especially for their patience during my low moments when I stopped writing for many months but still well understood when the time to keep on was possible. Same thanks to Blessings Christin Book Store staff in Calgary who guided me in choosing my publisher.

Thanks to Rebecca for her scrupulous care about this book. Her prompt review came when I needed it the most.

To all those who are willing to open their door for me in order to proclaim the power of the Gospel, God bless you. To all people who supported The Church of the Living God —Windsor, in Ontario, from 2005 to 2012. Thank you for giving me the opportunity to put the flag of the cross in that city. The seed you sowed by giving and serving will keep growing till Jesus comes back to take us home.

About the author

Eugenie Mukayiranga has been a dedicated Christian and evangelist for forty years. She has been a credentialed Minister in the Evangelical Missionary Church of Canada since October 2011. Originally from Africa, she spent eight years in Europe before moving to Canada in 1997. Eugenie was born and raised in Rwanda, a land infamously known for its 1994 genocide. This tragic event so deeply affected her that it caused her to question the meaning of life for a great period of time. Despite growing up in a peaceful and loving home, Eugenie always knew that an ethnic divide existed between the Hutu and Tutsi people. She did not however expect this unresolved discord between two tribes to lead to one of the greatest horrors of the 20th century. Being a sociologist by training, she understood in concept that man could reach unthinkable states of depravity. Nonetheless, this knowledge did not help her forgive those responsible for the terrible crimes committed in her homeland. Witnessing the willful extermination of so many innocent people left a deep and lasting sorrow in her soul. Then in 2001, she had an encounter with angels that helped her to read the entire Bible in an instant. Since that fateful encounter, she has come to understand that there is a kind of pain in life that only God, the Creator of the human race, can heal. Today, Eugenie volunteers as a community group leader at the Centre Street Church in North East Calgary, Alberta. She encourages people everywhere to pay close attention to and live by the principles of the Bible in order to rise above the biggest trial of all: Judgment Day. Eugenie now lives in Calgary, Alberta, with her husband and four children. In the Hopeland is her first book.

In the Hopeland
Even a Genocide Can Bring Life Back.

Intro: *This book is about the personal story of Eugenie Mukayiranga, a soul crippled by the Rwandese genocide then healed by two visions of hell. A short travel into the afterlife made her cherish the benefit of being a world citizen. She then made a decision to use her citizenship rights of free will for eternity's purpose.*

Hell is so real and very bad. Heaven also is real. Before dying, people must choose where they're going to go after death. A dead body cannot choose anymore. This book is an invitation for choosing eternal life in heaven instead of eternal suffering in hell. I have been there. In this book, I start by telling my short story of how I became a Christian, and then I share what I saw in an out-of-body experiences where I died twice, refusing to forgive the killers of hundreds of thousands of innocent people in my homeland of Rwanda during the 1994 genocide.

This book is divided into five chapters. The first chapter talks about the author, Eugenie Mukayiranga, a young woman living with the shocking reality of the genocide in her motherland of Rwanda. She was struggling and unable to forgive the killers of innocent people for seven years. From 1994 until 2001, her joyful nature had changed into a bitter one, until the time when she got two shaking visions about hell for unforgiving souls. As she says, it was like she was in a recovery room, praying that God would push death away from her until she recovered her loving heart. She did not want to die with sin.

The second chapter talks about Eugenie's struggle to admit that she had to forgive. She just had a vision of too many dead people in hell for the same sin she was guilty of. She was not able to overcome it until one of her old friends organized a month of prayers for that purpose.

In the third chapter, another vision following those prayers shows many souls of dead people held in unpleasant places of heavenly realm, far beyond visible planets. Then Eugenie, with fear of dying for good, found herself back in her body. She received the grace and ability to forgive all the people she could remember being mean to her. She kept that gift and uses it in her Christian walk today.

Eugenie knows firsthand that it is so hard to forgive. She understands that the price of sin is hell forever. She uses the fourth chapter of this book to show the unique chance that people still alive on earth today have in being able to use their free choice. Eugenie says that earth is the only land of hope for human kind. Because of her out-of-body experience, she is convinced more than ever that the Bible is so true: the inner man will live forever. The only way to have a happy eternal life for your soul, once your body decays, is to always keep your mind on God, repent, run away from sin, and obey what the Bible tells you to do.

Because death is so often unpredictable, not many people are really ready to die. The only way to enjoy life is to admit your sinful nature, repent, and accept forgiveness from Jesus Christ. The Bible gives clear details about life after death. The resurrection of the dead is a reality that only dead people can understand. For us, those who are still alive, we catch that meaning only by faith, supported by the resurrection of Jesus Christ Himself.

The gift of love from God gives Christians enough energy to keep spreading the Good News of life in heaven. God created people so that they can experience eternal joy in heaven with him. Adam and Eve ruined that goal, but Jesus brought it back. Only God's revelation can help people to understand that truth through the Bible in order to escape hell. No one should go there. That is the message the church keeps spreading until Jesus comes back to judge the nations, using his Word. My story from this book is one of many invitations encouraging people to fall in love with the message found in the Book of Life. It is about the unconditional love of God for his human race. His love offers freely eternal life with him in heaven. People should long and hope for it. For those who have it, nothing, not even genocide, can take it away.

For those who wonder if they should read this story, some of its benefits are detailed in the last three pages before the conclusion. It is a life changing story.

Chapter 1: In a Recovery Room of Grace for Seven Years

1.1: Born and raised with joy for life.

I was born and raised in Rwanda. I grew up in a loving Christian home. I received so much love and care in my childhood that now I easily give back that love to people I meet in life, when they want to receive it.

As a good catholic, I knew that heaven existed and that it was an everlasting home for good people. My way of getting there was to follow a saving practice of praying and going to church as often as I could. I also had to go and meet with my priest and tell him about my sins. The priest was the only person who had power to go to God on my behalf to get my sins forgiven.

I wanted so badly to go to heaven one day after my death. One reason for that deep desire was because I grew up away from my father. He left Rwanda to look for a job in Uganda and never came back home. I missed him. Later, I got to learn about an immortal Father in heaven.

Before leaving, my father let me go live with my aunt Anastasia Nyirabakiga, with an agreement of being able to go back home and spend every month of July with my family every year.

Here is why: my aunt had only two boys in their early twenties when I was a baby. She had asked my parents to give her one of their baby girls, if ever they would have some. The agreement for that gift was made long before I was born. When I was four years old, the time came for me to leave my family. I remember my mom telling me how I should behave in order to live safely in a foreign village where my aunt was living. It was very far from my hometown. Aunty Anastasia took me in and raised me. She was in her early forties and received me with great joy from finally having a girl of her own for the rest of her life.

Eventually, my dad came later to do official paper work for me being given away. He visited with me a few times before leaving for Uganda for good. To cover up for my absent father, my aunt told me about a powerful Father of all fathers up in heaven and that the only way to see him was to repent of my sins as quickly as I could all along my life until I died. That way, the door of heaven would always be open for me.

I was good in that routine until I was 17 years old.

In September 1975, I met some people at the new high school I attended that year. Three of them were young Christian girls. They took me into their group. Their love for God and for each other was contagious. They had a peace within them that shined from their faces. They could say anything without fear of hurting each other's feelings. Being the free and outspoken person that I was, these girls accepted my character so easily, and we are still friends to this day.

Right away, my new friends told me about being a "born-again". I laughed. They laughed with me. I only had a catholic background back then. The idea of being "born-again" was strange for me.

It took me a while to understand the meaning of new life in Jesus. Being saved or confessing my sins in public and witnessing about Jesus to others were all new concepts for me. I kept asking questions about those concepts until one day, in a youth Bible camp meeting, I understood. And then, I decided to be born again. I instantly felt the same peace my friends had. The joy from knowing that my sins were forgiven once and for all on the cross filled my soul. I invited Jesus into my heart. He has lived in me ever since, and he leads my path in helping others to repent of their sins and to follow him.

I received a Bible that day, and it has been my GPS (Global Positioning System), leading me to heaven forever. The words of Jesus inviting all people to him became my source of permanent peace. Jesus said, "Come to me, all you who are weary and burdened, and I will give you rest" (Matt. 11:28 NIV). I experienced that daily rest and peace in Jesus until, as I explain in the next pages, the Rwandese genocide sorrow took over my soul.

1.2: The Rwandese Genocide challenged my Christianity.

When I decided to follow Jesus, I joined people who were passionate about living out their faith and sharing the love of God with others, no matter what season of life they were in. Young or old, men or women, rich or poor, all the friends I made in my Christian journey were genuine, true, loving Christians. Sometimes, I encountered false Christians, I mean those whose actions contradicted their good teaching about Christ. I had no time to spend on them back then. I was told to only pray for them and to not imitate their example. I really needed to be strong in faith first, and then I could help others in being good Christians. I believe in the principle saying "you cannot give what you do not have."

Until the 1994 Rwandese genocide, I could go to bed every day with peace of mind. I could live out my joy and give out a message of hope to anybody, no matter what trouble life threw at me. By that I mean, since I was not easily offended, I was always ready to comfort others, no matter was kind of challenges they were facing.

The genocide in Rwanda happened when I was in Europe. My family and I were living in Strasbourg, France, when my homeland turned into a living hell. The government had pushed Hutu people to hate their Tutsi friends and neighbours. A million Tutsis were killed after being tortured without any remorse. We watched horrible scenes straight from our TV screen during the world-known "endless one hundred days of Rwanda". Some writers use this phrase when referring to the length of the 1994 genocide.

A number of good Hutu people were killed as well. Their offense was that they either looked like or tried to hide some Tutsis.

I will not give much details of my feelings during those one hundred days of hell my people in Rwanda faced. It is not easy to tell, and it brings back bad memories I try to escape in order to cope with life.

My heart was broken from a distance. I had no clue about my family members. The only news I had was that our beautiful house was destroyed by Hutu militia as soon as the killing started.

It took me a long time to get some news about my family. I lost my appetite and could not really keep up with normal routine of life. I was frozen by all the bad news I saw on TV. It was like an endless horrible time had come when the whole world was focusing on the shocking and worsening news about Rwanda. From April 7, 1994, a part of my real self died before my TV screen for endless days ahead.

In November 1994, I got the chance to go back to Rwanda. The killings had stopped. I received bad news about terrible things that happened to so many people I knew: killed, betrayed, tortured, disappeared, and more. In Kigali and in many other places I visited, including my own village, I could see mass graves all over the places. I saw so many dead body parts in the pathways that were crossed over by all the people passing by. I cannot find words to express what I saw and how I was feeling.

There were not many choices back then. Life had to keep going. The smell of death, trauma, and hatred was still around and freshly alive. I crossed paths with the killers of my people in my village, in the marketplace, and anywhere in town. I got mad at them sometimes. One day, my survivor mom told me to not keep going back in the village because I could be killed also.

I experienced the horrible feelings of survivors sharing about life with people who once "wanted you dead." Then I would crash into anger and scream to the killers I met. Jails in Rwanda could not contain all of them.

Some people in my village had done bad things to my own family members, to my friends, and to people that I knew very well. To see me there was like a nightmare to them. I could see a deep fear and guilt in their eyes. When I asked them why they did these bad things, many of them turned into preachers to me saying that "only the devil can do such things," not them! So most of the killers were living in denial, putting the blame of the genocide on the demons, and not accepting it themselves. From that experience, I decided to help people be more responsible for their choices. I saw that the concept of sin and evil can be twisted in such a way that can give right to all evil doing in mankind.

During the six weeks I spent in Rwanda after the genocide, my heart was so broken. My loving personality turned into a hateful one. I could not love or forgive people easily anymore. All the horrible stories I heard made me bitter. The most hurtful stories came from unexpected sources. I could not handle hearing about the bad things done by people I expected it from the least: my neighbours, those I grew up with from my young age, and those whom I loved very much all my life. I quickly learned how they turned into great killers of innocent people. When we met, it was very hard for me to stand their cold, guilty look.

Some genocide survivors told me details of everything they went through. *It was not easy to forgive people from what I heard they did.* I remember crossing some fellow and asking him, "Why did you try to kill so-and-so?" He proudly responded that I should be thankful to him because he could not kill all of them. Yes, thanks to God he could not, but plenty of the survivors were still living the nightmare in orphanages and in psychiatric centres of Rwanda. They are still carrying a life of loneliness inside of them because no one can repair their broken past. Only hope in God's miracle keeps them alive. In January 1995, I returned to France.

About two years later, in February1996, I went back to Rwanda. I was trying to find a cure for the horrible heavy pain deep in my soul. People were searching all over the place, trying to find dead bodies of family members and friends in order to bury them properly. I did my part. Then I kept trying to understand what had happened in the mind of the killers. The more I tried to find that out, the more I got sick of it, to the point of almost losing my mind.

The most comforting part was meeting with some old friends. Sitting together, hearing what they went through and how they still had hope in the future brought a priceless joy to my heart. But I was unable to help them out because I had to go back to France after six weeks.

My three kids, aged between 7 and 4 years old at the time, were waiting for me. My youngest, Lydie, was sick of me being away. She was put on antibiotics any time I was a week away from her. The oldest, Jo-Victory, later told us that because he saw so many Rwandese dead bodies on the TV screen, anytime his dad or I was not yet home by evening, he thought we were killed. He carried those worries for a long time in his child-hood. He was eager to learn how to make food for himself and for his younger sisters in case his parents were killed. The girl in the middle, Rebecca, was quieter and too young to tell her feelings, but she could feel sad from time to time without a clear motive.

Three years later, I moved to Canada with my family on April 6, 1997. Was it a coincidence to land in the wide peaceful country of Canada on the third anniversary of Rwandese genocide, one of the worst world *human failures of the end of the twentieth century?* Only God knows.

Following the advice of one of our new Canadian friends, Sister Judith, we settled in St. Catharines, Ontario. Three years later, our family became bigger. We were blessed with our beautiful millennium-born youngest girl, Sarah.

I was still angry with the killers of my people. I was also mad at the international community for their lack of empathy towards Rwanda during the genocide. We moved from Europe to try to find peace of mind on another continent. Back then, in my mind, it was better to leave France. It is said that it had compromised too much in the Rwandese genocide. To this day, it is still not clear whether France could have done things differently.

Even then, I was still deceived by some mean people who were close to me, and who knew my daily pain of not being able to forgive them. Their careless attitude was another way of keeping their horrible deed alive in me for a long seven years, waiting in pain to hear them say "sorry". That never happened and moving to a different country was not healing my pain.

My growing kids needed a joyful, smiling face from their mother. I had to pretend again and again. Today, those kids are grown and happy, and they love God and people. I praise God for that. They may still remember some of my changing moods of that old time. *A long-lasting pain always leaves scars.*

In fact, that pain was adding to a deeper one I already had preceding the genocide. I had lost so many relatives starting in 1990, when the war started in Rwanda, ending in a 1994 mass genocide—the only one known worldwide for being shown on TV from the best channels of the world. The mini-genocides destroying many families had been happening in some villages, away from the media. For example: I was born in Kibilira commune in the North of Rwanda, a few months before the first genocide started in 1959 in Rwanda. My grandpa's home was put on fire, leaving the whole family homeless. My mom remembers very well how a Hutu family—"kwa Nyaramba," she says—took her parents in, hiding them safely until they could build another house. That was more than half a century ago. Today, what the e-newspapers call "the massacres in Kibilira commune in October 1990" is another one of those unspoken genocides in Rwanda.

Daily, I asked myself how I could be set free from my ongoing agony deep in my soul. My Christian background kept me feeling guilty of sin. According to the Bible, I had to forgive all the people who caused my suffering as soon as possible in order to have assurance of meeting my Heavenly Father one day. I had to leave all my worries to God, the right judge for all. However, my sorrow *suffocated the faith I had in God and in the Bible.* What I saw and heard about my Rwandese people suffering *made my eyes on God so blurry* that I could not really see or feel his comforting hug that I used to experience in my dark moments before the 1994 genocide.

The only thing that kept my hope for better days was this: I never doubted God's love for me. I never doubted his power to deliver me from pain. I was just failing to wait on him and his secret timing in action. From that period of time, I learned *that patience in time of trouble is the most challenging* moment in life. We all tempt to rush and find our ways out from an unpleasant situation. It takes strong support from God to not make bad decisions coloured by the challenges of the moments.

1.3: Hope keeps our dreams alive.

I knew from the Bible that God exists and gives reward to those who seek him (Heb. 11:6). That truth was my spiritual oxygen of the moment. As long as I believed that way, I could not die with the sin and sorrow of an unforgiving soul. I knew from the Bible that "the wages of sin is death" (Rom. 6:23). I also knew that hell is for sinners and that eternal joy in heaven is for people who repent from sin daily. But I could not help it.

Every time I thought about those who committed the genocide, I knew I did not forgive them. My daily prayer for those years was to ask God to help me forgive them. That was also my prayer request I asked my Christian friends to pray for me. Some agreed to pray for me. Others were quick to preach to me, saying that because I was a Christian, it should be easy for me to forgive. Knowing the truth does not make it happen right away. Taking positive action about it is a path toward freedom.

Those who caused my hurt never apologized to me. But as soon as I reminded them to recognize their own faults, they kept mocking my attitude and saying things like "what kind of Christian is this lady? So what, she is not the only one hurt in life. She should keep quiet and just move on. Life is hard for all of us."

My Rwandese culture teaches us to *remain mute about personal problems.* Rwandese people are supposed to look very cool from outside. Expressing your struggle in life is looked upon as a weak character. Because I am and enjoy being emotionally expressive, I have always been a strange Rwandese person that way. Call me awkward, weird, whatever—I will enjoy who I am instead of playing or pretending to be who I am not. Being real brightens my days. For me, hypocrisy means betrayal. As a human, I can use it only in extreme necessity.

Before the hurtful events in 1994, I could easily forgive and forget. I had always carried the peace of God within me. For that reason, I knew the difference between a clean conscience and a guilty one. I knew I needed to be able to love and forgive everybody, but I could not. *I had a soul crippled by the Rwandese genocide. I needed a healer. I needed a specialist for wounded souls.*

I knew one thing: by trusting God and doing what is good before his eyes, I was trying to behave as his good servant. That way, I knew that his eyes were always on me.

1.4: A heart of a servant pleases his master.

I kept serving God during hard moments, while waiting for his intervention in my anguishing life.

During my time of sorrow and resentment, I kept being nice to people, but I let them know that I was still hurt. I kept serving God as a good Christian, but I was not really satisfied because I was not used to carrying sin in my life every day. I was not able to preach on forgiveness during those dark years of my life. It was a time when all Rwandese people were so broken that we had to help one another in order to survive. It was also a time where I had to be careful to follow God's voice telling me what to do. It was not safe to follow my own feelings.

My heart could hear the whispering of the Holy Spirit telling me to forgive everybody, but I just kept blocking my conscience about it. I used to respond to God like this, "God, you know that it is hard, that I am suffering, that those people really did wrong to me, that the fault is for those who do not apologize knowing that they hurt me," and so on. The list of excuses was getting longer and longer every year. But something kept me connected to God. I could not forgive my enemies, and I did not hide that sin from God or from men because I've always hated a fake appearance.

I kept obeying God as much as I could in serving him and serving people. My love for God in that way did not change. I think that is how I kept my door open for him to touch my life and keep using me in preaching the Gospel. I knew that serving God the way I could was the only way to get my wounded soul healed one day. It was in that context that I went to visit one of my old friends who really needed my support. It was a long journey for me, going very far from home. It required a big sacrifice, but I was so happy to do it.

1.5: My Heavenly father visited me while I was doing good for him.

If you want to see God at work in your life, stay in his way: His way is his will. He is busy saving people from the power of sin. His way is found in his field, in his vineyard. (Matthew: 20: 1-16).

Wherever and whenever we are meeting people's needs, God is there with us. His love pushes us to live it out by helping others. The Bible says that "For Christ's love compels us, because we are convinced that one died for all, and therefore all died. And he died for all, that those who live should no longer live for themselves but for him who died for them and was raised again" (2 Cor. 5:14–15 NIV).

Whenever we are teaching about God's plan for people, whether by words or actions, we are becoming God's extended hand on earth. This way keeps us more satisfied and less concerned about our own unfulfilled needs. Paul also said in 1 Corinthians 1:31, "Let the one who boasts boast in the Lord." When we stop complaining about our own problems and work to make other people feel happy and loved, we let the glory of God shine around us. Then we can notice miracles happening in our life at any time.

In the next pages, I share with you three miracles God used to deliver me from my seven years in pain.

1.6: The first miracle: A voice from God while I was serving him.

The beginning of my deliverance started with a voice of promise from heaven. In June 2001, I was living in St Catharines, Ontario, Canada. I was with my family, and we had gone on a long trip to visit a friend in the United States. We were so happy to do this. It had been on my heart to see this visit take place. My friend and I had been asking God's help for a serious matter. I will not give details about this simply because it was my friend's business, not mine. I can only say that, in many ways, on that day, God had just answered prayers we shared with that old friend from a very long time. *My heart was in a mood of thankfulness.*

On our way back home, I took a break from driving. My husband Esdras was now behind the wheels. The kids had school the next morning, so we had to be home as early as we could for them to get enough sleep. It was late in the afternoon. We were about to cross the Detroit, Michigan border. Then, from nowhere, I heard a quiet voice telling me that God himself was coming to help me to forgive people I could not forgive. This voice said, "I have given opportunity to your closest people to help you, but now I am coming myself to do it." Then the voice stopped. Please remember that my husband was driving. I looked at his face to see if he heard that voice. I saw that nothing had changed because he just kept driving as usual.

Then I asked, "Did you hear someone talking?"

"No," he said.

Then I said, "God just told me that he is coming himself to help me to forgive."

"Wow, okay," my husband said. Then he started to rejoice saying, "Oh, God knew that no one else can help you for that. I am glad he is coming to do it himself."

From nowhere, deep in my soul, I was convinced that the voice was from God. I know from the Bible that the Holy Spirit living in the heart of a born-again Christian can convince us about the voice of God in our mind. Jesus said, "But when he, the Spirit of truth, comes, he will guide you into all truth. He will not speak on his own; he will speak only what he hears, and he will tell you what is yet to come" (John 16:13 NIV). He also said how his sheep hear from him in these words: "My sheep listen to my voice; I know them, and they follow me. I give them eternal life, and they shall never perish; no one will snatch them out of my hand" (John 10:27–28).*

---

* Let me be clear: Anybody can hear from God. He, the maker of mankind, knows how to tune our mindset to the channel of his voice. He has been speaking to men and women in different ways, but mainly through the Bible, his Word. If anyone wants to know how God speaks, there are plenty of resources and church leaders who are ready to teach about that. "Gotquestion.org" is one of many websites which offers good answers about God and the Bible.

From that day, I started to rejoice, expecting God to come Himself and help me to forgive. I did not really know how and when that help would come. But I had unshakeable faith in that voice from heaven.

By the end of June 2001, I traveled back to Quebec City, where I had been doing my studies in sociology. I had a very good relationship with God at that time. I was praying for God's direction to be able to help a group of Christians in planting a church in that city before I finished studying. My gratitude goes to the senior pastor of All Nations Full Gospel Church from Toronto (www.anfgc.org/branches), Pastor Samuel Donkor, together with Pastor Veronica Adu-Bobie, who supported my calling and opened a church there. That church is still alive today. It is called All Nations Full Gospel Church International (ANFGCI), led first by pastor David Nitonde. The leadership was passed to pastor Protais Nyandwi a few years later. This happened a little bit before the time I got my visions from God about hell.*

Again, I was doing God's work when a second miracle was about to happen. During a normal quiet night, I slept as usual. When I woke up, I realized that I had an unusual dream: I had a vision from God. After that, I knew that I had to be more

---

* It is usually a great pleasure for true Christians to be able to leave a place of worship wherever they go. After helping people to repent from sin, we encourage them to join other believers in order to know more about obeying God and serving him in the community. When the believers grow in number, they are advised to start a church that will keep helping people around that place to follow Jesus. That is what I was doing in supporting the group of Christians I met in Quebec City from the year 2000. That is what God wants believers to do anywhere they go spend some time. That is what the first disciples did wherever they went.

serious and find a way to forgive. But I was not yet able to do so. The next chapter gives details about that dream.

1.7: The second miracle: A vision of unforgiving souls held hopelessly underground.

In the next few pages, I give details about my vision of an angel showing me the Bible and a little bit of hell for people who do not obey what the Bible says. This was my first out-of-body experience.

It was a normal night at the end of June 2001. I went to bed, and then in the middle of the night, *I had a dream.* Out of my burning body, an angel of God took my real self out of the fire, and we went together underground.

To understand the next story, remember that this vision occurred during my sleeping time. I took my journal and wrote that dream right when I woke up. It is not easy to know how long the dream took to finish, simply because I cannot tell when the dream started. I used to sleep from 11:00 p.m. to 6:30 a.m.

While sleeping, the dream started as follows: From nowhere, I found myself in a party or a meeting held in a big room on the first floor of a tall building. Many people there were happy to be together. I remember recognizing one of them, my old friend from Rwanda whose name is Ebralie; she now lives in Nashville, Tennessee

[Let me say something about my friend. As a teenage girl, Ebralie always had an easygoing spirit and easily connected with people, loving God and others. From the first day I saw her, her smiling face has been a source of joy for so many people around her. Recently, I asked her what makes her sad or how sad she felt during the genocide, and she responded, "It is hard to describe or even understand how we survived! All our friends are gone. It is hard to make new friends! God only knows why he protected us." She told me that she is living extra days. She calls life after the genocide "bonus days."].

Now let us go back to my dream story. In that dream, as soon as Ebralie saw me, she ran toward me with a big smiling face. She was expecting me to help her recover and to bring her peace and comfort. We had been away from one another for many years. We really missed each other. She started by praising God for reconnecting me her. She also reminded me how I used to comfort people, and she wanted me to do the same thing for her at that moment.

Unfortunately, I started telling her how things had changed for me, how my passion diminished, and how emotionally wounded I had been for what had happened in Rwanda. I started to go into details about bad things people did to me and to my family in Rwanda. My friend was surprised because, knowing me as a strong believer in the past, it would not have been a big deal for me to forgive those people and move on in life.

While I was telling her my struggle, her peaceful and joyful face started to change. I could see how my story was taking away her joy, and I remember now how (in my subconscious), the Holy Spirit's voice was telling me to change the subject and to tell her good stuff so that she could still keep her joy. But I refused to obey what the Holy Spirit was telling me to do. I kept saying bad things about people who really wounded my soul. She knew most of them.

23

All of sudden, from nowhere, we saw a spark of fire catch the carpet of the floor where we were. Fire spread quickly, burning everything in its way. Everybody in the room ran in all directions, fleeing the fire. Everybody escaped but me. I was burnt from head-to-toe, along with everything I was wearing. I felt the pain of burning with all my senses still alive. First, my clothes burned, and then my flesh completely burned until I died. But something within me could neither catch fire nor die. That was the real me, my soul. I knew I had just died in the fire, but my intelligence and my conscience remained untouched. Wow!

Instantly, my intelligence and my conscience were in another kind of body and had another ability to cross over and to understand a little bit about life without an earthly body. Out of nowhere, *an angel came* to show me the way to go after death. I knew that I was a dead person from earth, but I had forgotten the pain of fire I experienced just a few seconds before. *My body had died, but my soul was alive with a sound mind.* I realized that we were going to explore the underground life. I was expecting to go up into heaven when I died, so I was not happy to be going downstairs. The angel kept leading me down into another world that was apart from earth. When I got to this destination, I found a clean basement with many rooms and lights in it. The area was completely locked *without any exit possible.*

Before the angel left me, the same angel took a big Bible *as if from thin air—I mean, from God's mind.* He then opened it slowly three times in such a way that I could read every page of the whole Bible in less than a minute. While the angel was opening each page of the Bible for me to read, I was able to see and read and quickly understand all the verses talking about unforgiveness. All verses about unforgiveness were outlined in big and black bold letters.

A mini judgment was happening before the eyes of my soul. I was so *deeply sad* in a way that I cannot describe.

After the third time of opening all the pages of the Bible for me to read, the angel closed it and pointed to the room where I was supposed to enter. Down there, I obeyed without any power of opposition.

I, hopelessly and very sadly, realized that my sin of unforgiveness had condemned me to go down there for the rest of my life—I mean, for eternity! I could feel eternity as a strong feeling, like I could almost touch it. I could not speak to the angel. *Not only was I sad for my horrible condemnation, but I was also sad that I could not come back to earth to tell people how the Bible is so real.*

The pain of not being able to come back to earth or to send the angel or another person to tell about the destination of sinners was a terrible pain that I wish no one to have in life. The other kind of pains I had in life on earth were temporary. I could bear them knowing that there is an end to everything on earth. The hope I was carrying on earth was helping me to cope with any kind of pain or any sort of disappointment. But the kind of pain I felt after death was *a hopeless pain*, a permanent pain, an eternal pain.

Knowing that back on earth, where I just came from, thousands of people play with sins without repentance and knowing how death came so quickly to me, I knew that the same thing could happen to anybody on earth. My sense of a loving heart, my passion of celebrating people changing from bad to good, and my love for a repenting soul on earth was still in me. But there was no way out of there to come back and at last give one warning about hell to people on earth. It was a cruel and useless desire of doing good because there was no way of doing whatever I wished to be doing. I knew that the *time for free will was over forever. WHAT A HELL!*

Right before the angel disappeared, *something (the Spirit of God commands in hell, too)* told me to turn back. Instantly, I had the ability to turn my head and look back to a higher underground area but facing the direction I was coming from. I was able to see very clearly thousands and thousands of people who had died the same time as me. (Ten years later in 2011, a Google search showed that there are an estimated 151,600 deaths each day, with 6,316 people dying each hour, 105 people dying each minute, and nearly 2 people dying each second; www.ecology.com/birth-death-rates. Back in 2001, I was not at all familiar with using Google or thinking of statistics about people dying every day. The website above was still unknown to me).

That day, from underground, I saw an ocean of people coming down towards where I was. I looked at the angel to see whether he could feel my pain and take my message to earth to do what he could to warn people who were still alive about *missing the point*—that is, *missing the opportunity to go to heaven.* The angel disappeared right away. I could not see him anymore, and I was *left on my own but with the ability of knowing where to go.* I turned my head and went to the room the angel had showed me to enter. Before entering, I saw another room. It was half closed, but I could tell that some people were inside with some secular music playing loudly. I passed that room and entered the room on my left.

I saw that everybody was dancing and singing so loud secular music, boys and girls together. It was almost like a night club. No couples were there. I understood that everybody had recovered life before marriage. Everybody was single and not even thinking of getting married. Everybody had recovered the status of being single.

Among many people at the party, I saw and recognized one person: a man in his thirties. *I will call him Copain.* I knew him on earth, and I know he is still alive today. I barely thought about him before my vision. Right after the dream, I urgently searched for him until I was able to have a talk with him about his spiritual life.

That fellow named Copain recognized me and shouted that he wanted to dance with me. He came *out of the crowd* to invite me to dance. I refused, saying that I repented from enjoying secular music. He insisted.

When he saw that I was not going to accept his offer, he naturally rejected me and invited another person.

I got an understanding that down there, selfishness prevails. The sharing system is unknown to them.

That fellow was not really surprised by my refusal, maybe because he already knew that I was always involved in church activities when we were still on earth. It is *so sad that I kept my Christian convictions there but could not and had no ability to practice anything I loved to do on earth.*

There were other rooms close to that one, with many young people ready to get invited to dance. My fellow was so popular there already, surrounded by people who wanted to dance with him. When that fellow saw that I was like a stranger there, he took time to tell me what was waiting for me.

He said, "Eugenie, you better dance and relax a little bit for now because there is a special treatment waiting for you and for other people of your kind." He added, "People who did not live a Christian life on earth are friends of the chief of this place. We are daily worried badly for the Judgment Day. But at least our boss here does not bother us because we share the same nonstop pain and fear. But for people who, on earth, were holding Bibles and saying the name of Jesus, even those who said that name once but end up here, they get special treatment morning and evening. The chief of this place has an army. He delegates two soldiers for each one of your kind of people. They will take you every morning and every evening. They will put chains on you and bring you away from us and beat you badly every day until the Judgment Day. There is no mercy for people of your kind here."

Then he went on to tell me that people like him, those who did not live a Christian life, got along with the boss down there and shared the *horrible fear for the Day of Judgment*. That is a permanent but traumatizing memory for everyday life for people who died and joined the underground life. **I got it.**

I got to understand the unending painful hopelessness of people who die without Jesus on their side. I tasted a little bit of a permanent but traumatizing memory for everyday life of people's souls who run away from God here on earth until they pass away. I thank God that I died with Jesus on my side. The death in my dream could not hold me down there. There is a verse in the Bible telling all believers "Even though I walk through the valley of the shadow of death, I will fear no evil, for you are with me; your rod and your staff, they comfort me. You

28

prepare a table before me in the presence of my enemies. You anoint my head with oil; my cup overflows" (Ps. 23:4–5 NIV). Those words became mine forever.

But back then, after that explanation, the sorrow of a desperate and nonstop hopelessness invaded my soul. Remember that I was out of the dead-burnt flesh of mine. Eternal condemnation but also permanent suffering away from God became so real to me in such deepness that no words on planet earth can explain. Why? Because there is always a possible way out when we are still on earth, whether it be for real or by dream or plan. *I was in a world without possibility of decision.* The worst prisoner on planet earth was way better than me down there. At least, even though that prisoner is still in jail, he still has a way of free-will and choice.

When I woke up, I had so much fear. It was still night, and I did not know where I was or whether I was alive or dead. Then I slowly recovered my earthly senses, got out of my bed, put the lights on, and looked around to convince myself that I was still on earth. I tried to drink water to see if I was alive. I swallowed it, took a deep breath, and then **realized that I had a vision**. *I knew that I was given a story to tell*: This was a message from God about hell for people on earth who still doubt the truth of the Gospel.

I sat down on my bed, took a pen, and wrote the whole story in my daily notebook I had in 2001. I still have the original manuscript, and you can recognize it because it was a hand written in two languages: mixed with my native language, Rwandese language for 99 percent of it and some French, my second language. I had spent only four years in Canada, so I was still struggling with English vocabulary at that time.

After that, I called my husband and told him about the dream and asked him to keep praying for me so I could forgive people easily and never end up in the kind of place I just saw.

That was my second miracle, after a voice from God had spoken to me three weeks earlier. It was a push up from heaven, helping me to obey God and forgive my enemies.

Chapter 2: Wrestling to Choose between Life and Death

An immediate forgiving spirit would have been an immediate choice for life. If I didn't do so, I knew that I would be on the path towards death and eternal torments like what I had seen underground in my dream.

After the vision I had about eternal punishment, I really did not know what to do. Being angry at the "bad guys" had been a pleasure to me. That attitude was helping me to keep balance between the sorrow in me and the desire for revenge that I was not ready to act on. Now that I had seen hell waiting for me, I had to decide which side to take.

It was neither easy nor clear why and how to obey the Bible and forgive people who had hurt me. Knowing that God was not happy with me did not help me to obey him. So I kept slowing down going through life. But I became more willing to share my sorrow and my experience about hell. I was even ready to help other people choose God's will, while I personally could not. I also kept asking God to help me to obey him and forgive. *The hardest test was to wait for his timing.* But I still shared about angels, the Bible, hell underground, and so on. I kept telling people that the Bible is so true, even though I could not do what it was telling me to do.

2.1: Some lessons from my first out-of-body experience.

The vision of traveling in another world as a dead person is not common among the living. We all have questions about dying and the afterlife. For myself, dying and then find out later that it was not for real, that fact alone added a tone of faith to what I believed about life after death. The Bible made more sense to me after that vision.

The understanding I got from that dream helps me a lot in spreading the Gospel. The passion I got for the Great Commission has not left me ever since. Now that I am back to on earth, my deepest desire is to help people get their life right with God. I always look for people who recognize and promote the idea that there is a God, that he is the creator of all of us, and that we have to love him and glorify him by obeying him in our daily various walks of life.

In the dream, I had intense feelings in my soul and mind apart from my body. Even though I had been burned and was completely dead, my spirit, my conscience and emotions were still intact, sensitive and perfectly sharp and smart. I could understand that I died and left the planet earth forever. Those feelings will stay in my memory for life.

From that experience, I realized that there is a high level of understanding when you're out of your body. Our fleshly nature stops us from catching the spiritual meaning of things here on earth and beyond.

I understood, once and for all, the painful reality of people condemned by God for eternity. Those are people whose goals in life are something other than loving God and his creation.

Those are people who strive to be loved and appreciated by men instead of by God first. One of many scriptures that talks about those people this way is John 12:43–48: "For they loved human praise more than praise from God...."

I was also sad to see that none of my friends were in that underground life. Since the angel showed me where to go and left me, I entered into a hopeless place. Then, the selfishness took over my soul. I wished to have friends to share my suffering in hell. My soul could not be happy anymore. I was sad because I found myself in a world that enjoys things I repented from a long time ago and *I would have been forced to do things that I trained my soul to hate.* I was sad because I would no longer be among people who loved the same stuff that I loved and who hated the things that I hated. I was condemned to stay in a place that was not my type of environment at all on earth before I was burned to death. I was so sad because I knew that there would be no *way out from there **ever.***

If I had a choice, I would prefer to go back to earth and do my best to follow and obey what the Bible said. (Remember that, in this dream, I had died by fire in a building.) The feelings of burning to death and leaving earth were like a drop of water in an ocean of pain that I felt during my short experience of the underground life. ***The pain of never again being able to change my destiny was the real death for me.***

The pain of hell is real. It is palpable. It is tangible. Once in hell, the endless pain is clear. There is no need to prove that hell is painful beyond comparison for people who get there. In my case, what was killing me the most was not being able to come back to earth, to my life, not even for a second, and give a warning to people about hell.

Anyone who reads this story can imagine the joy I felt when I awoke from this vision and realized I was still alive and had the opportunity to share my experience. Being judged by the Bible in hell gave me more joy and energy to share it for the rest of my life. May God open more doors for me for that reason alone! He can also use you in sharing the Gospel and change nations wherever you are. If only you believe it.

In the underground life, there was no sense of time or desire for sharing the Gospel. I normally have so much empathy for people that I was sad at the thought of living with these selfish people forever.

That place is part of hell: The person living there keeps fighting an unending sorrow inside of himself knowing that the scripture condemning him or her is fulfilled for eternity. It's a place without hope, a place with an unending painful state of living soul and spirit aware of the terrible Judgment Day to come for *eternal condemnation.*

There were no feelings of unfairness about staying there, though. For some reason, the new mindset of the soul without its body understood the decision of God. I could tell that each person knew that he deserved to be there. *No one was blaming God for being held in hell forever. Oh how God is the unique sovereign judge!*

Let me also clarify this: Out of my body in this vision, no one had to tell me a word. I just knew about the next steps. It is like God gives order to all souls instantly, and the soul gets a very quick understanding from God's language, especially when the earthly body gets detached from the soul and spirit. The Bible is true in saying that "things that come from the Spirit of God…are discerned only through the Spirit" (1 Cor. 2:14). In other words, only people who died to self can easily follow God's direction! The Bible also says that "Those who belong to Christ Jesus have crucified the flesh with its passions and desires" (Gal. 5:24). And the Apostle Paul said this: "So then, brothers, we are debtors, *not to the flesh, to live according to the flesh.* For if you live according to the flesh you will die, but if by the Spirit you put to death the deeds of the body, you will live" (Rom. 8:12–13).

I am a witness to the fact that *our bodies hinders us from understanding the spiritual world.* I can also testify that only people who choose to obey God and the Bible while they are still alive here on earth can live a happy spiritual life after death.

But after this first vision, I was not able to forgive just yet. I was pondering between my will and God's will, between my way and God's way. The flesh I live in was still attracting me to the human nature, and it still does. It is a permanent fight for choice between good and bad, clean and unclean, true and false, and so on until the last choice between life and death.

I cannot buy the lies of theories denying life after death. I believe that there are *two major forces of life: the good and the bad.* There is what God agrees with and what he disagrees with. God takes the side of people who, during the struggle of life, are eager to do good no matter how many mistakes they make while trying. God comes in that trying time. I agree with what Google tells me about Benjamin Franklin in what he meant two centuries ago, saying: "that knowing is better than wondering, that waking is better than sleeping, and that even the biggest failure, even the worst, most intractable mistake, beats the hell out of never trying."

The Bible teaches and encourages all people still alive today to choose their permanent residence with God in heaven now. The other choice takes you to hell forever. I saw it. None of the living should go there. It is hell to go there. ***It is hell to go to hell.***

We should never separate ourselves from what God likes. That separation is the hell the Bible warns us about. For me, because I was surprised by unexpected death myself, in my vision, I think the saying that "it is never too late" should be replaced with "now and only now" is the time to make the right choice for eternal joy with our Heavenly Father. Why? Because it *can* be too late. The Bible tells us that "God will judge his people and that it is a dreadful thing to fall into the hands of the living God" (Heb. 10:30–31).

I agree with the Bible's that "now is the time to choose God's side." Let me give you a few examples. Mark 13:36–37 urges us to "watch because God can come to take us home anytime." We read in Hebrews 4:7 that "God again set a certain day, calling it 'Today.'" This he did when a long time later he spoke through David, as in the passage already quoted from Psalm 95:7–8: "Today, if you hear his voice, do not harden your hearts."

We find so many warnings in the Bible about being always ready to meet with God. In 2 Corinthians 6:2, we read this: "For he says, 'In the time of favor I heard you, and in the day of salvation I helped you. I tell you, now is the time of God's favor, now is the day of salvation.'" Another scripture says, "Do not boast about tomorrow, for you do not know what a day may bring forth" (Proverbs 27:1).

These verses have power over me now. But it was hard to accept them and obey them right after that first vision of hell. All my senses were still *paralysed by the anguish* from the genocide in my motherland. The pain inside of my body—from what I saw and heard—was crying louder than the pain inside of me crying for peace and joy from God. My earthly senses for revenge, or at least for keeping hatred toward the trouble makers in Rwanda, were still alive in me.

The dose of hell I saw and felt was so real while I was out of my body. *Getting back into my body took away the shocking reality of hell.* I had to admit my weakness one more time and ask for help in order to make the right choice. But this time I was serious. I had tasted a little of the painful destination waiting for the *unforgiving crippled soul of mine.*

2.2: Knowledge is useless until applied.

After that revelation, I went on wrestling to choose between life and death.

I spent three months struggling for a choice between either God's way or the highway of my choice. Choosing God's way was to remember what the Bible says about loving our enemies. This brings life and opens the door to eternal joy. It can eventually bring our enemies to repentance. Jesus tells us to never seek revenge because hate is sin and brings death.

After that vision, I realized that I was almost dead for good! I was now convinced about the best choice for me: **to forgive**. But *thinking that way did not make it happen.*

I was not really dead to my own desires. It was not easy for me to accept giving up on my personal right, to wait for the people hurting me to apologize first and then I could forgive. I knew that my attitude was contrary to the Bible, but I could not help it. I knew that "it is a sin before God to know about the good thing to do and not do it" (James 4:17). My knowledge could not help me. *My free will was stronger than my knowledge.* That attitude made me so stubborn that I could not hear the gentle whisper of God's voice, full of wisdom.

Later on, I understood that people who do not fear God and those who are not eager to live in holiness cannot easily apologize. The truth is that each one of us can hurt people without even noticing it. It takes the grace, revelation, empathy, and gift of humility from God to be able to do so. In my case, it was my duty to get right with God and to forgive unconditionally in order to face my final day with real peace. That day can occur at any time for real for each one of us. But at that time, I needed help in order to be able to apply that knowledge. Knowledge cannot save us. Applying it can. That is why some Christian friends decided to organize prayers for me. They were asking God to make a way for me to obey the Bible as soon as possible.

2.3: The power of intercession: God hears prayers of his faithful servants.

By the end of September 2001, I reconnected with Laetitia Murekatete, a very good friend of mine. Before that, the last time we had really spent time together was in 1984. After so many years, I did not even know that she had survived the genocide.

I was so happy to hear from her again. A long time ago, in Rwanda, we had been together in the same high school, back then called Lycee Notre dame d'Afrique-Nyundo. There, we had also shared Christian life activities with a few other

Christian teens. We had a very real happy high-school life together by the end of the 1970s.

By the time we reconnected in 2001, she was living in Belgium.

Before that, while I was visiting Rwanda after the genocide in December 1994, I had crossed her hometown of Ndera. I was bringing a genocide survivor to the Psychiatric Centre of Ndera, a few miles from Kigali, the Rwandese capital city. At that time, that centre was full of people who had lost their mind, traumatized by what they went through. It was so very sad and frustrating to not be able to help much about that.

As I was passing by her town, I remembered how I used to go for sleepovers with Laetitia's big sister Kayitesi Modeste in the mid-1980s. The last time I spoke with Kayitesi was on the phone. She was in Paris, France, for a visit. She had a very good life standing as a long-term faithful worker of the United States Agency for International Development (USAID) in Kigali.* Few months later, she got killed during the genocide, together with a lot of her other family members.

---

* About Kayitesi Modeste: Ambassador Margaret McMillion unveiled a plaque honoring the twenty-eight mission employees. The plaque reads: United States Mission Kigali, Rwanda. IN MEMORIA André Karani Jean Nepomuscène Nicyolibera Aloys Hakizimana **Modeste Kayitesi,** Donath Mutuyeyezu, Theophile Kazungu, Eugène Nyirumulinga, Médard Mwumvaneza, Marc Bizimungu, Come Rusimbi, Edmond Bizumuremyi, Francois Mugenzi, Telesphore Ndayambaje, Andrew Gasana, Damien Mivumbi. Godelieve Kagoyinyonga, Félix Mupenzi, Pierre Claver Mulindahabi, Clement Sebera, Thaddée Ruzirabwoba, Emmanuel J. Kayitare, Pierre Gatera, Joseph Murangwa, Eugénie Mujawamariya, Viateur Rwamasirabo, François Ntaganira, Augustin Munyambonera, Celestin Nangwahafi. U.S. Mission Employees killed during the genocide and war in 1994. May your souls rest in peace. WE SHALL NEVER FORGET YOU. (Source: United States Department of State, October 2003, *State Magazine,* pp.7).

All those memories pushed me to pass by her parents' house to see how the family was doing and the beautiful house I knew before. I was shocked to see only a bush and the rest of a destroyed property. From that time of December 1994, no one told me what happened to that family until I spoke with the survived sister Laetitia in 2001.

I knew that if she was still alive, she had to tell me if and how she was coping with life after the genocide. It did not take a long time for her to tell me about her struggle and her hurts after losing a lot of people among her lovely family members. She told me how she was able to forgive all her enemies. The story was interesting and encouraging, but I could not catch it really. I did not get how she was able to be so free, happy, and able to love everybody again. She told me her side of the story and explained to me how she was helped by a good pastor and a good loving church and how she had special people—prayer warriors—praying specifically for her deliverance from hate and hurt. She told me that I needed that kind of prayer. Then I asked her to pray so the same thing could happen to me.

Having been where I was, Laetitia took my request very seriously. She promised that she would contact her Christian friends and ask them to pray for me, saying my own name before God every day for a month. I was happy, and I trusted her. For once, someone had heard my cry after so long! What good a friend can do! And guess what happened—God heard! Her prayers were answered. My friend's intercessor group moved the heart of God for me. You are about to read what happened to me next.

Thanks to the Ambassador M.Margaret. My respects to all victims whose memories will never be known.

Chapter 3: The Third Miracle: An Encounter with the Heavenly Realm and Principalities, My Second Out-of-Body Experience

In the process of helping me to forgive my enemies, God gave me another miracle. *He gave me another vision of punished soul held in the heavenly places, in an eternal, hopeless, painful life, with no way out.*

An angel of God took me to see the residence of satanic principalities beyond the sky. In the Bible, the Apostle Paul teaches us about the bad spirits fighting against us. He wrote: "For we are not fighting against flesh-and-blood enemies, but against evil rulers and authorities of the unseen world, against mighty powers in this dark world, and against evil spirits in the heavenly places" (Eph. 6:12). What I saw beyond two levels of the heavenly realm gave me a **hint** of where and how principalities from hell were holding people's souls.

The angel also showed me what to expect if I kept postponing my time of forgiveness. Right after that vision, I received the grace to forgive instantly, and I kept that gift.

One of the main goals of my story is to renew the awareness about the Bible, the book ready to be used on Judgment Day for all nations anytime soon. I saw that book twice in my visions when I died and came back to life! I wish I could have had a camera and put a *big picture of the big Bible being opened by an angel and myself without a body, reading it to my soul.*

Another goal is to tell about how important it is to keep forgiving people who hurt us. The Bible is so clear about it. There is no other strict formula than the Bible's command about it. I finally understood that truth that we all fail to obey so many times. I will just share my experience, hoping that some people can get benefit from it, as I did myself.

3.1: The heavenly realm with principalities from hell is real.

I went to bed as usual during the night of September 23, 2001. Then I had a vision. In the dream, I found myself in a place looking like a flat circus. I was with my family enjoying a variety of games.

All of a sudden, *out of nowhere, something unknown **unexpectedly** happened,* causing *so much chaos* that people in the circus were scattered all over the place. I could see people shooting guns in the crowd. I was helping my husband and kids to fight the fear and run away safely in order to survive. I was even telling them how we should not fear death because it is the way to heaven for us as Christians.

The gunmen kept shooting. Some of them were clothed in military uniforms and others in casual clothes. They got to me and started shooting at me multiple times. At least ten bullets hit me, and I died. I knew that I was dead after the last deadly shot. Before I died completely, though, in my agonizing short time, I started to sing one of the secular songs I knew from before I was born again. That song is known in the French community as "On ira tous au paradis," by French singer-songwriter Michel Polnaref. That song says that "we will all go to heaven, whether blessed or cursed, Christians or Gentiles," and it tells people "Do not be afraid of the color of the flames of hell." I had not sung that song since 1976, when I was born again. So until 2001, that song was in my mind for twenty-five years without me thinking about it.

I was *physically dead in this vision,* but *my real self was intact.* My conscience remained happy, singing the same secular song, boasting that I am going to paradise. I had no worries about my dead body at all. From that day, I see my *body as an envelope covering my real self in order to only serve God.* The scripture telling us to guard our hearts more than anything else makes more sense to me ever since.

After leaving my body, from nowhere, I saw an angel putting two wings on me. Those wings were very long and big. They were connected to the real me, the one who could not die, the one killers can never reach, the real self: my soul. I saw my body lying on the ground in a bush close to where the shooting started. It was not moving anymore. That empty body of mine was still being shot very badly. Then the angel stayed on my left side. I saw that he had the same wings as the ones he just put on me. We then travelled up toward the sky together. We were using our wings to go up with a smooth but kind of fast speed like a big bird, an eagle, or a plane flying at slow speed.

While they were shooting my body after my soul had left it, I could not feel pain. I did not really care about it until I looked down on earth. I could see very well. I saw that the bullets used were like foam of soap coming off the guns. I was also able to hear what they were saying about me. They were so mad at my body, saying that I was bad and because of that, I had to be killed. Their boss was explaining how I was known to attend prayer meetings regularly. *The gunmen were mad at me because of my way of loving God and teaching people how to love him and how to care for others. Those are some of the accusations I heard leading them to shoot me to death.*

Remember that I could see and hear that scenario happening on earth while I was already way higher in the sky. Then we kept flying.

Before I could go higher beyond the sky, I looked down on earth one more time. I saw my husband and my kids going their way peacefully, away from the gunmen. I did not feel the pain of missing them or the fear of never seeing them again. I never thought about friends, siblings, houses, cars, or any other belongings I had cherished on earth. My mind was different from the mind I had on earth. *I had no worries about earthly things anymore.*

I was still singing the same secular song and happy to fly with the angel. You will see how a secular music did not do any good to me.

The angel never talked to me. I had *spontaneous knowledge* with a clear mind that I must keep following him!

We both kept flying. Then we crossed beyond the sky, crossed at least two levels of the places up above, beyond the seen physical world. Those levels were so large that my mind could not capture their size. I did not see what kind of living or material things were up there; but what I could tell was that the heavenly realm is so huge that a normal human brain cannot catch its size. Then I entered the third level. I kept going higher.

Remember: I was still singing my secular song, even when I was halfway up the third level of the heavenly realm. All that time going up through the heavens, I could see the bright side of the vast heavenly realm.

Then all of sudden, I stopped flying up. The angel was still on my left side but never talked to me. Somehow, all that time out of my body, I just knew *what to do next without a visible leader*. In less than a second, I saw that I was going lower toward my right side.

For the first time up there, my senses became more aware. I started to get worried and stopped singing my song about paradise. I kept flying lower and lower and slowing down. The space started to turn darker and darker but never got completely dark. I had enough light to see my surroundings. I opened my eyes carefully enough to see what was going on in the lower places under me *but still beyond the sky*. I was born with a curious mind, and it seemed I died with it at that time.

Then, through that kind of semi-darkness or semi-bright area, flying lower, I could see a huge metal barrel made in very thick, silver material. That barrel was open and was as huge as the largest gymnasium you can imagine, larger than a stadium all round. I could feel that, somehow, the heavenly realm was divided into specific departments. The thinking I got was telling me that the area I was flying over was a place made for those huge barrels. I could feel that explanation in my conscience and understand it without reading any signs about it. My human senses in the spiritual realm were so powerful, precise, and clear. Because of that, I have no doubt that human spirit has something about God in it. We are really, according to the Bible, created in His image.

I was able to see inside the barrel. It had at least ten people in it. It was so huge that the people looked very small in it. I saw that each person was standing very close to the thick walls of the barrel, and they were all very busy doing the same thing. Each one had a smaller barrel in front of him or her. The people there had no gender, male or female, everybody looked exactly and perfectly the same.

Those smaller barrels weren't metal. In my mind, they looked like a wood mortar, similar to those used to grind some cereals or cassava roots into powder here on earth.

But, in the dream, the understanding I got was that the mortar was bigger and stronger, ready to *be used, nonstop, for centuries of years ahead.*

Each person was holding a thick stick, crushing some kind of seeds very hard to turn them into powder. I understood that those people would do that kind of job for eternity and that I was supposed to join them and do the same job *forever and ever.* When I understood that, I got so sad and felt hopeless. That endless hard job of grinding seeds in a barrel was so annoying. To stay with those people keeping silent and supposedly never helping each other was *a horrible place to spend eternity.*

Further on is displayed a miniature form of a wood mortar and the stick used in some food processing. My gratitude to the Karangwa family who gave it to me in December 2013 when I visited them. I am using my two pictures to mimic the last image I saw in my mind before waking up from my dream.

Once I woke up, I choose the attitude represented by the picture on right. I this book context,. I choose to forgive, recover my peace and move on, instead on waiting apology from people who may not even know bad things they do to me. If needed, I can reduce my interaction with them in order to keep my joyful spirit.]

I did not know whether those barrels were supposed to get hot in the evening or at any time when the leader of that place wanted them to. I had that question in mind when I woke up. I was almost getting there, imagining that my feet could get hot in there. I saw the spot that was supposed to be mine. I seemed to understand that someone would give me the same material as what the other ten people had and that *I was not supposed to talk to them for eternity.*

I was kind of standing in the air watching that scenario in my mind. I tried to see clearly who those people were—their faces, their color, their bodies—to see if they were male or female. I could not make out any difference. Everybody looked exactly the same. They were not wearing clothes like on earth. Their bodies were dressed in a brown striped fabric. It was as if someone had drawn that pattern-style identically on their body, with brown oblique lines followed by some light dark lines successively from the head to the toes in such a way that no one could tell the difference between those people. Does this have something to do with tattoos in style these days? I do not know, but some of them remind me what I saw up there.

While I had so many questions in my mind, some unseen being interrupted in my thoughts and said with a *slow voice* "*Do you see how you make a difference between people on earth? Here, we see everybody the same way. There is no way of telling the difference between people by looking at their bodies alone. They all look the same here—no male, no female, no specific colour. They are all the same. It is a waste of time to focus on differences between people the way you do it on earth."* In my mind, I felt like saying, **"I get it!"** I was not allowed to talk. There was no social life up there, contrary to the social life we have on earth, or the one I had seen three months before in the underground place. My intelligence was so high and quick to catch the meaning of things and any information needed up there.

All of a sudden, *out of nowhere*, the same angel who had been traveling silently with me all along the trip in heavenly places took *a big Bible.* I did not see where that Bible came from. It was as if an *unseen instructor* kept leading all activities there. The angel opened the Bible before my eyes, three times. That action was done so professionally and peacefully that I could read every page of the Bible from Genesis to Revelations. I had the ability to recognize all verses talking about forgiveness. All scriptures about my unrepented sin were in big and bold printed letters. Those words were so easy to read that I had no excuse about not knowing their meaning. My intelligence was so high that I could catch the meaning of anything in less than an earthly second!

3.2: A human soul is made for spiritual understanding.

When talking about God's judgment of sin, the Apostle Paul says that our conscience will be our judge before God through these words: "Even Gentiles, who do not have God's written law, show that they know his law when they instinctively obey it, even without having heard it. They demonstrate that God's law is written in their hearts, for their own conscience and

thoughts either accuse them or tell them they are doing right…
God will judge everyone's secret life" (Rom. 2:14–15 NLT).
Those words became alive to me that night. I also realized how
true another verse Paul wrote is, "God will give eternal life to
those who keep on doing good, seeking after the glory and
honor and immortality that God offers" (Rom. 2: 7).

Once again, I saw that outside of our bodies, each person gets
a supernatural understanding of things in a way that does
not happen with our brains here on earth. I could instantly
remember very well when and how I did not forgive so many
people after the genocide in Rwanda. I could have a quick revelation about what the Bible was telling me. I could not talk to
the angel, but I knew that the judgment happening to me was
right and perfect. I was hopeless but still wanted to find a way
of warning people back on earth about the truth of the whole
Bible. I wanted people on earth to know what happened to
me, but, like in the first vision, *there was no way out of there.*
The angel was not ready to hear me or go do send that message
for me either. Today, I know that all heavenly power relies on
the tasks of the Holy Spirit sent to earth to do the will of God
through us.

What a hopeless world! What a tormenting place! That experience was more painful than anything in my life on earth. I
wished I could send the angel to earth to tell others, but he
was not talking to me the whole way. Also, that angel looked
so disciplined that he could obey only the *unseen instructor*
anyway. It was clear in my mind that he was not there to please
me nor to accomplish my wishes.

When the angel closed the Bible for the third time, showing
me that it was time for me to go to my spot for my permanent

boring job, before he took wings from me, I woke up. *This was not fun.*

I wish I could have a picture of me hanging in the air of the third level of heaven descending down in the barrel. I remember that as if it happened yesterday.

3.3: Back in the Hopeland, an ultimate care from heaven.

When I woke up, I did not know where I was, I could not find my angel, my wings, or the place I had been flying. I did not know whether I was on earth or not. I was so sad and afraid and wondering if I escaped my condemnation! I opened my eyes. It was still night, and I was lying in my bed at the Canadian Université Laval in Quebec City. Working on my PhD in sociology there could not help in understanding the spiritual realm surrounding me nor heal my suffocating, wounded soul.

I then, slowly put my night light on, got out of my bed, put the big light on, opened curtains to see outside, went back and forth, turned back to sit on my bed, got up again, got a glass of water to convince myself that I am still on earth and that I can eat and drink and have normal human senses. I finally realized that I was still alive. What a relief! I still had a chance to choose and correct my ways of thinking and doing things! **I could still catch the hope we have here on earth!** I did not know that the killing brokenness from the **genocide could bring my life back!** I was a stranger to death because of Jesus who heard my cry of seven years! **I was meant to live forever. No wonder! As part of the human race, —I belong to eternity.**

By this time, my memory started to play a nonstop wrestling match. I took a deep breath. I realized that I had received a vision from God because there were activities going on with an angel and the Bible involved in that dream. This was not the first time I received revelation from God, but it was the second vision I had where I found myself in a hopeless place after my death during a dream. I also remembered the vision I had three months before in June 2001, when I ended up in hell for eternal repeated punishments among all the friends of the devil. I cooled myself down and grabbed a pen and a notebook to write everything I remembered about the vision. I had to do that as soon as possible. This has been my habit about dreams from God.*

I was not sure whether I would get another chance to survive another sudden death. I had to be very concerned about my sins and run away from them before it was too late. The Bible, in the book of James 4:7, tells us that resisting the devil will make him flee from us.

I was so sad about missing heaven for the second time within such a short time that **I repented right away**, forgave every person I knew of who did wrong against me, and was able to **instantly forgive everybody I met on my journey to heaven.** I learned that forgiveness is **not only a command but also a gift from God.** It comes with Jesus when we accept him as a saviour in our heart. I learned that refusing to forgive is the same as literally refusing to let Jesus to reign over us. No wonder I could not reach heaven when my soul left my body.

---

* My hand writing can be shown to anybody today for both visions and other revelations I got from God during the same period of time.

If I had handed all the hurts and sorrow from my soul to Jesus, I could have gone straight to heaven the first time I died. Instead, I chose to keep remembering all the wrong things from the Rwandese genocide. I will always praise God for his grace in allowing me to come back to life twice.

Later on, I got some understanding about my second chance. Since I had chosen Jesus Christ as my saviour, he gave me another chance. I realized also that death could not keep hold on me since I believed in the power of the blood of Jesus. There is no other way for me to understand how and why I came back to life twice. For that reason, I had to use the second chance I freely received. I had to surrender all to God and be totally dedicated to him, the Bible, and the cause for Christ.*

---

* I am free from hate forever. Only God, through Jesus, can grant the freedom of true love and set us free from hate. From the time I got free from hate, so many people have been testing my love for God and my ability to forgive, more than before. They purposely try to push me to get mad at them and hurt them back. When I realize that they do that repeatedly, I *understand* that they are hurt and that they choose to release themselves by hurting others. I then try to engage conversation with them, alone or in a group. If they avoid talking about their problems, I have to avoid them as much as I can and pray for them from a distance. I let God deal with them. Only God can change people who love to freely hate others.

Shari Scott convincing me to put my story in a book.

I laughed and she laughed with me.

Mukayiranga Eugenie

Then we agreed.

Above is our house after the genocide in December
1994- a piece of the wall of the living room

Below is our house in December 1994, ruins of
our kitchen, bathroom and storage room:

Ruins of our house, whole view in December 1994

Ebralie in the 1980s

Ebralie in Nashville USA today

Laetitia, in the summer 1984, with her husband
Jeremy in the streets of Brussels, Belgium

Laetitia today.

* The picture below is of the late Modeste Kayitesi on her wedding day.

Pictures by Photo Studio Calgary // www.photostudiocalgary.com
**The picture on left: I imagine myself unhappily grinding uncrushable seeds forever.
**The picture on right, I imagine myself happily grinding crushable seeds for a short period of time.

Chapter 4: Personal Commentaries: When God Gives a Vision, He Also Gives Understanding

I cannot tell in detail everything I learned from those two visions. I trust God to inspire and reveal himself to anyone who reads this book. In the next pages, I will give some of my understanding from what I saw during my afterlife experiences.

4.1: Earth is the only land of hope for human kind.

I came back from death twice. After the second vision, I was so frightened by the hopeless world I just came from. My heart was beating so hard with so much fear from facing eternity with unending sorrow. Coming from a miserable world with no way out was so meaningful to me. I understood right away the priceless value of being alive on planet earth. I hope that these few pages will stimulate each reader to take the opportunity to be right with God before death comes. I was born and raised free. I cannot fit in a world without choice. Now that I can choose, I have to look for people who willingly want to spend eternity with God in heaven.

The Bible was the only book the angels used to put me in the place I deserved. The Bible is the ultimate book that gives the best approach for *a happy eternal life with God in heaven.* It is a powerful thing to understand the resurrection of the dead for eternity. I got a glance at eternity for real while I was still on earth. That is the main reason why I was motivated to share my story. I wish everybody could get an eternity view on life, the same way God does. His grace can make it happen to anybody now.

4.2: Our mind should long for the permanent connection with the presence of God.

> Avoiding distraction and remaining focused on God's will have been my way of living ever since my out-of-body experiences in 2001.

When I woke up from those two dreams, I knew that if I was close to God, if I had a forgiving heart, if I was using the power of the name of Jesus truly, I could have gone to heaven. I recognized that I should make my spirit and mind always ready to meet Jesus any time he tells his angels to come and bring me home in heaven.

> For the eternal well-being of our inner man, our life requires principles and practice. The Bible gives all we need to know about how to have a happy eternity. It is called our spiritual food. Jesus said, "It is written: 'Man shall not live on bread alone, but on every word that comes from the mouth of God'" (Matt. 4:4).

The same way healthy food improves our body's functioning, so does the Bible for our spiritual life. If we want to live with God forever, we have to purposely enjoy walking toward our happy ultimate destination.

> Since September 2001, one of my new resolutions has been to immerse myself with the Word of God and to hear from the Holy Spirit living in me, until I get thoroughly saturated with the presence of God in me and around myself. In other words, I have to make sure that what I am doing and planning to do is for the glory of God.* Even though I normally make friends easily, I do not make a lot of friends among people who long for their own glory.

After those dreams, I took two years calling people who had hurt me and apologizing for my unforgiveness during that long period of time. At the end of each conversation, I asked them to get saved, find a good church, and grow spiritually in order for them to go to heaven after this earthly life. I still do

---

* I am passionate about telling people to get their soul and spirit prepared to receive God's love. The book *The Pilgrim's Progress*, by John Bunyan, has passed the test of time. Churches have so many others resources that they do not talk about that book as often as they did in the 1980s when I was a new believer. But now there are easier versions to read and even movies based on this book. It is among the best Christian books I recommend for anyone who wants to refresh their mind about always being ready for the journey from this world to the one that is to come in heaven. That book shows a very good ending of life for whoever wants to have a joyful afterlife experience with God in **eternity**. A bad ending for careless people is shown too.

the same almost every day and will do so until my last breath on earth. Once I forgave, there was no need for an apology.

Even though I do not request an apology before forgiving people, I still get worried for people who cover up their mistakes and try to hide or deny them. If they do not ask God's forgiveness, they will not enter his holy place. The Bible tells us that holiness, through Jesus Christ, is a requirement to get to heaven. Repentance and confession open the door to forgiveness.

4.3: Our body puts limits on our spiritual being.

After those visions, I better understood how our body limits our spiritual understanding. As I said earlier, the second vision allowed me to see a little bit about the *spiritual realm above the earth and beyond the sky*. From up there, out of my body, without binoculars, microscope, or other optical instruments used here on earth, I was able to see down on earth—how earth is so small in comparison to all things that God created around it! Oh how wonderfully and clearly my eyes could see what was happening on earth from such a long distance in the sky! God is all-powerful. I will never have enough words to explain how much our body puts limitations on our spiritual senses and abilities.

I was convinced more than ever that I had to repent every day for the rest of my life on earth. I have to do that as much as I can remember, read my Bible often, and get right with God according to the Bible. I realized more than ever that it is not enough to be busy preaching and singing in church to get to heaven. I was convinced that there are no excuses to give to God to avoid judgment when we refuse to give our sins to Jesus in order to be forgiven and receive righteousness through Jesus Christ alone. The Bible is so real when it says that for God "to obey is better than sacrifice" (1 Sam. 15:22). The whole chapter of Samuel 15 shows how the flesh led Saul into disobedience and how God rejected him as king.

4.4: We have to always be ready for our journey after death.

Let us not be caught off guard. Death came to me when I was enjoying anything but holiness. The song in my soul was proof of that the moment when death surprised me.

In fact, when I thought about what happened to me in the second dream, I was mad at myself for singing a secular song until I was almost perishing. It is not a bad thing to enjoy secular music, as long as we get right with God. There are so many secular songs out there that give great meaning to life in general. But what I know from experience is that the willingness and attitude of being right with God will push a person to enjoy music after knowing that the meaning of it gives real peace in the soul and that it is conforming to the scripture pointing to eternity with our Creator God in heaven.

Before that vision, I did not know the benefit of always having an attitude of thankfulness in my time of joy and sorrow here on earth. My destination after death would have been different if I had trained my soul to enjoy the presence of God in me all the time. I willingly kept sorrow and unforgiveness in my soul for so long that I disconnected myself from the will of God. I kept following only my own feelings and socialized easily with angry people about the genocide in my country instead of choosing to connect with people who forgive others easily.

The Word telling us to not tempt God is so true. We should never push God to get angry. We better not. *That is one of the reasons I apply the verse of James 1:12–15 to my story* and it leads me in everyday life to do my best in obeying God as quickly as I can. It says: "God blesses those who patiently endure testing and temptation. Afterward they will receive the crown of life that God has promised to those who love Him. And remember, when you are being tempted, do not say, 'God is tempting me.' God is never tempted to do wrong, and he never tempts anyone else. Temptation comes from our own desires, which entice us and drag us away. These desires give birth to sinful actions. And when it's allowed to grow, it gives birth to death."

4.5: Death is mostly unpredictable.

I was also convinced more than ever that human beings have a high chance of getting caught by death as instantly as some other events that happen to us daily. That is why it's so important to always be ready and repent every day. It is not natural for us to think about getting ready for death. However, we see people passing away every minute of every day. The Bible tells us many times to get ready to leave this earth anytime for the Day of Judgment will comes like a thief in the night (see Matt. 24:32–44 and 2 Peter 3:10).

Knowing that truth had been helping me to ask God to not allow death to get me before I could forgive. It was my prayer every day for 7 years, every morning and every night. I thank the Holy Spirit who was my reminder all along those years. He is still doing his job at all times, until my last breath.

4.6: Let us give ownership to God concerning our daily living.

> We should live a Christian life peacefully but with such seriousness that no one or nothing should draw our attention toward another motive other than the Kingdom of God. I do not mean that preaching the Gospel is the only job God wants us to do. Like Jesus on earth, we have to dedicate all of our activities towards what he wants to reveal through us. In other words, he wants ownership over everything about us. He is also the best support even during our worst moments in life.

We need to have unshakeable faith in the master of life. Since life goes on after death, our free will has power as long as we are still alive here on earth. It is a matter of choice between joy and sorrow forever. Our daily life points toward one or the other side of life. Our conscience about that principle should be always turned on Jesus, the one mighty to save.

4.7: How can we always be ready?

The love, faith, peace, and hope promised and given to Christians the first day they believe should help us to live with a confident and trustworthy attitude in the action Jesus Christ accomplished on Calvary for all human beings. And we should be confident knowing that if we obey the Word of God, we will make it to heaven. The Apostle Paul encourages us to trust Jesus in our daily walk with him in Philippians 1:6: "Being confident of this, that he who began a good work in you will carry it on to completion until the day of Christ Jesus."

Joining a healthy church or a team of Christian friends is one of the best ways to keep going until we reach our destination. Individualism or self-sufficiency should have no room in Christian journey.

4.8: The journey to heaven is not about routine; it is about creativity.

Because every minute is different from the previous one, God is always creating new things and new opportunities around us. Before having those visions, I was only preaching the Gospel and paying some attention to the needy people around me whenever I wanted to by simply showing love the way I could. Since the time I had these visions, I am now more focused toward God's goal in life. Every person I meet matters more than before. We all face life or death every second of our being on the earth. Also, every minute and every second in life can make a big difference in our destiny, depending on what kind of choices we make. I pray and do my best to reach out to unbelievers for Christ. I have decided also to work with teams whose goals are to lead people to true repentance and acceptance of Christ as their saviour. I also follow up with the spiritual growth of Christians around me whenever possible, always having in mind that prayer with faith can change things for the better.

4.9: Surely our body will decay, but our soul will live forever.

My out-of-body experiences revived and restored my under-standing of the words of Jesus that tell us that we should not fear those who kill the body but to "fear him who, after your body has been killed, has authority to throw you into hell. Yes, I tell you, fear him" (Luke 12:5).

Through my experiences, I better understand now that our souls will never die. We should stay away from teachings that deny the afterlife in eternity. One of the main goals of the Bible is to give us a precise roadmap for eternal life in heaven. The resurrection of the dead is such a serious matter that we should never ignore it. That truth caused lots of trouble espe-cially when the apostles started to teach openly about it, but no one can change anything about it. Denying the truth does not make it false.

4.10: The free will and free choice we have on earth have an end.

According to my first vision, as I wrote before, there was no hope for me to have another choice than to obey underground forces and regulations. This truth was the same with my second vision going with the angel of God up beyond the sky. Only the will of God reigned over the place, telling angels what to do with me. The gift of freedom given to mankind is unique and should be used properly.

On earth, we have a choice. Out of earth, we no longer have a choice. Any animal on earth has more freedom than an after-death human soul. In other words, because Jesus is the only way to heaven—and heaven is the fulfilment of our joy, peace, and freedom—there is only freedom in him and him alone. So we *should use our free will by following Jesus's path daily. Jesus is the only way to be and to remain free forever.*

4.11: Looking at a multitude of lost people in a second has put a permanent mark on my soul.

I believe that true love brings people to enjoy life and to desire to keep living for eternity. Therefore, the meaning of a heavenly life forever can only be understood when life on earth makes sense. And life on earth cannot make sense when there is no continuity of it. That is why the Bible makes sense for human kind for yesterday, today and forever.

After my out-of-body experiences, I became more concerned about the quality of the church today. My visions pushed me to really examine the way the mission of winning souls for Christ is being done in today's world. That mission is about helping people get ready for heaven with God after they die. Since my visions, I now understand better than before how each day becomes too late for almost 150 thousand people who leave the earth every day. The nonstop **throng of perishing people from all races** I saw that night showed me the truth of hell. I cannot ignore. No one should.

My visions and revelations from them gave me a deep desire to share my story with people who read this book. My expectation is that after reading it, people will be more determined to get ready for life in heaven before their time for choice is gone with them.

My hope is that people will be more attracted to reading and obeying the Bible, the only book that will judge us for eternity.

A healthy, loving community is what matters the most in life. Only a good team of believers or a good church can prepare people to get ready to go to heaven at any time they die. Some Christians today enjoy hurting each other instead of lifting one another in love. We have to go back to the root of Christianity where other people's salvation and spiritual well-being matter so much to God, the same way ours does. That way, doing life together will have a healthy and joyful meaning every day.

Church gatherings that turn into a selfish, self-love attraction or a business lifestyle cannot focus on a heavenly life where everybody is supposed to live out life sharing everything in love. Neither prosperity nor people-pleasing and miracle-promising can buy salvation. Jesus paid it all 2,000 years ago. Unto him we owe all.

I knew that unprepared people can perish and go to hell, but then I saw it with my own eyes! That gave me a whole new purpose in terms of disciple making. It made me bold in telling the truth about sin and forgiveness through Jesus Christ. It became easier for me to speak about eternity with God to anybody I can reach before death takes over.

4.12: The great majority of people are not ready to die.

From my experience, human kind is not ready to die. Living in the flesh makes us blind from God's sight. Thinking of the Judgment Day is not in the mindset of the majority of us here on earth. After we die, that idea only remains and keeps bringing fear in the souls of people who are not ready to die.

Today, I am still alive and happy because I believe that *Jesus refused* that the devil and death to keep me underground. I came back to life because I had permanent faith in Jesus the one who conquered death on the cross once for all. Even if I am a sinner, I hate sin. Sin can catch me by accident. I do not plan it because I am always ready to leave this planet. According to my faith, only those who truly give their life to Christ are happy when they think about death. Christianity is the only answer to the fear of dying.

In the Bible, we find the meaning of life: the resurrection of the dead and spending a happy eternity with God made possible by the only one who made it, *Jesus Christ. For me, that is the unchangeable truth of all time.*

Jesus is the only one who rose from the dead and came back on earth to invite us to go and spend eternity with him. He told us that there are a lot of houses in heaven for all who will believe in Him. (John 14:2).

Please try to understand the first miracle that took place right at his death: "Jesus, when he had cried again with a loud voice, yielded up the ghost. And, behold, the veil of the temple was rent in twain from the top to the bottom; and the earth did quake, and the rocks rent; And the graves were opened; and many bodies of the saints which slept arose, And came out of the graves after his resurrection, and went into the holy city, and appeared unto many. Now when the centurion, and they that were with him, watching Jesus, saw the earthquake, and those things that were done, they feared greatly, saying, Truly this was the Son of God." Matt 27:50-54. We can all get our life back after death, if only we trust in Jesus now while still living. *The only way of getting ready to die is to plan to live.*

4.13: Why two visions when one was already enough?

The answer to this question is simple: In the Hopeland, our loving God always gives second chances.

Between those two visions, I knew the right thing to do: to forgive right away. But I kept arguing with God. Who was I to keep reasoning with God? I learned that we should neither reason with God nor lie to Him.

I knew that the Bible said, "For the wages of sin is death, but the gift of God is eternal life in Christ Jesus our Lord" (Rom. 6:23 NIV). I kept admitting that I needed help until the help came in a form of a second out-of-body-experience, with enough power from God for me to be able to forgive.

The second vision helped me to better understand the power of pain, the power of God in heaven and in hell, the spiritual realm forces, the power of the Bible, the function of angels, the power of prayer, the everlasting life of our soul, the powerlessness of death, and the tormenting Judgment Day in hell. God knew my weakened faith and the right dose of grace I needed. For that fact, I trust him more than before in all things I do.

4.14: The power of pain and the price of revenge.

Sad events can be deadly because they can turn us into enemies of God. There are so many hurts in this world that cut deep into our soul. The genocide in my country of Rwanda was one of those kinds. I was wondering how God could keep the killers of innocent people alive. I wished them dead, too. But that is not what the Bible teaches. It says that the desires of revenge bring hell. *The horrible pain inside of me was screaming in my mind louder than the soft whispering voice of God.*

I learned that we should never let our circumstances talk louder than the Word of God. When we feel sad, we should not hide it. We should not blame it on God either. Instead, we should pray and ask for help until the joy comes back. It is not easy to hear from God when we are upset.

Not obeying God and not forgiving people was making me a lukewarm Christian, the very thing that God hates. The Bible is clear about that. It says in Revelation 3:15–16, " I know your deeds, that you are neither cold nor hot. I wish you were either one or the other! 16 So, because you are lukewarm—neither hot nor cold—I am about to spit you out of my mouth." NIV. We have to find a way of dealing with pain before it turns into bitterness.

The pain in my soul kept me in the wrong for seven years.

There is a high risk of hell for a long-term sinning behaviour. I felt I had the right to feel rage against people who killed so many family members and friends in Rwanda. That long-term sinning attitude of my heart drove me to the path of an unrepentant life. *Sin should happen only accidentally* and then be quickly but sincerely repented as soon as possible. The Bible says, "Therefore confess your sin to each other and pray for each other so that you may be healed. The prayer of a righteous person is powerful and effective" (James 5:16).

One of the signs showing true repentance is that, if a person has done something wrong in the past, he can talk about it in a past tense as something already forgiven and forgotten by God. Usually, there is no shame or guilty feelings about it anymore. The past forgiven sin and failure should become a powerful lesson, and smart people learn from their past mistakes. That past also becomes a testimony about the power of God in the life of a sinner when he recognizes Jesus as his saviour and righteousness.

4.15: The authority of the Bible and the service of angels.

The two angels holding the Bible and helping me read it through carries a meaning that shows the authenticity and the authority of the Book of Life. The angles I saw were in charge of bringing dead people where they really belonged, using the Bible.

When angels showed up suddenly after my two experiences, I knew instantly that I had to obey them. I knew that they had a mission to lead me into the other world of life, out of earth. I did not expect to see the Bible in their hands! ***That was and is still the biggest surprise of my whole life.***

The fact that angels in both of my visions of death used the Bible to show me where to go and why I had to go there has increased my trust in the Book of Life more than ever before. The words shown to me from the Bible were so true about my life on earth that I had no argument against them. Reading them alone convinced me about the justice of God toward me and about following the orders of the angels without any other choice.

For me, getting visitation of angels from God twice showed me that *the heavenly government is well organized* in taking care of the souls and spirits of the dead. They know very well where dead people belong after death. They also have a way to let the dead person know where and why he is heading to the good place with joy for eternity or to the bad destination with sorrow forever.

The power of the Book of Life is real. Being *judged through the Bible* during my *out-of-body experiences* has helped me to give ultimate value to the **Holy Bible** and to be bold in telling people to read and obey it in order to know and apply what God wants for them. Before those visions, I was doing the same thing but not with the same passion and boldness as I do today. Also, going through the spiritual realm back and forth has helped me to understand the *power of prayer* and the *authority of the name of Jesus over all spirits* on earth, underground, above the sky and beyond our understanding. I feel like I'm talking to the real and almighty loving God. Since he released me from the power of hell, I owe him all that I am and all that I have. I have to use all that I can to help other people know him and love him intimately forever. If the *heavenly government* is so well organized for dead people, how much more is it for the living creatures? There is no question about a heavenly angels' organized activities, schedules and shifts regarding life on this planet earth. Think about it!

4.16: The discovery of the power of God in hell.

After my first dream going underground, I realized that *God commands everywhere, even in hell. The mind and power of God is beyond our imagination.* According to my earthly thinking, what I saw after burning and dying with fire, the angel, the Bible, and all that I saw came from nowhere. But when I woke up, I understood that they were from the mind and the command of God. In the Bible, Jesus recommends that we always ask God to match our will with his will from heaven (see Mathew 6:10). He knew that only what God decides matters and comes to pass.

The spiritual realm requires a spiritual system and spiritual math and spiritual understanding. The spiritual realm doesn't count the time like on earth. Time is a thousand times faster, and the intelligence or understanding ability of the soul is a thousand times higher than when we still wear our physical body in this world. In 1 Cor. 2:14, Paul explains that things that come from the Spirit of God ... are discerned only through the Spirit.

4.17: We have to make sure that our name is in the heavenly registry before we die.

If there is a book of eternal life in heaven, there might be a book of eternal death in hell. If men can easily make record of a variety of activities and events, is it not much easier for *God to keep record of his creation?* The Bible says, "For we must all appear before the judgment seat of Christ, so that each of us may receive what is due us for the things done while in the body, whether good or bad" (2 Cor. 5:10). Also in the book of Revelation 20:15, it says, "If anyone's name was not found written in the book of life, he was thrown into the lake of fire." And again, we read in Hebrews 9:27–28 that "Just as people are destined to die once, and after that to face judgment, so Christ was sacrificed once to take away the sins of many; and he will appear a second time, not to bear sin but to bring salvation to those who are waiting for him."

I knew what the Bible said about a sinner who does not repent. I believed in the existence of hell, but I never saw people in hell before my first out-of-body experience. What I saw led me to stand on this: *If men have records or registry services, what about God?*

This understanding became my motivation in everything I do every day. Meeting desperate and hopeless people in hell helped me make more sense of what Jesus said according to the Gospel: "There will be more rejoicing in heaven over one sinner who repents than over ninety-nine righteous persons who do not need to repent" (Luke 15:7 NIV).

Winning souls for Christ should lead our goals in life. Any activity we are involved in can be explained according to the Bible. We can all use talents and expertise we receive through life for what matters the most in life, leading to our future life with our Creator in heaven forever and ever. Deleting names from the book of hell should be the passion for a true follower of Christ no matter what we are called to do here on this temporary planet earth. *There is always joy in winning.* Winning eternity and living with God, through Jesus Christ, is the ultimate reward. Let us all strive for it until we make sure we win it before dying. I thank God for that awakening vision.

4.18: An expectant attitude toward God pays off.

God answers prayer. He answered my daily prayer and for the prayers of those who prayed for me. The year 2001 *was my year of jubilee*. I had just spent twenty-five years walking with Jesus when I was delivered from the pain inflicted by the genocide in Rwanda seven years earlier. And I was finally able to forgive.

The sorrow can come back especially in the month of April when Rwandese communities get together to remember and to help each other be strong and hold on life. The sorrow also can come back when something happens reminding me a little bit of the hard past times we went through as a people. But the difference is that I do not hold a grudge against specific people. I can easily tell that I received God's comfort because there is no more anger behind that pain anymore. Since God does not show favouritism, he can do the same for anyone who asks in order to do things right. One of many scriptures about that is in Acts 10:34–35, when Peter said: "I now realize how true it is that God does not show favouritism, but accepts from every nation the one who fears him and does what is right."

I learned also to never doubt about God's care for us. I was convinced more than ever that he hears our cry, our praises, and our prayers. Paul's command to us is *to pray without ceasing* (Thess. 5:16–18). I saw the answer of my seven years of unceasing prayer.

Deliverance from God is available and free of charge; the only price is to keep walking in obedience to him during the period of time that we are waiting for his answer.

Chapter 5: Being Pragmatic.

When I am telling my story, some people ask me questions. It may still be the case now that I put my story on paper. After reading this story, some people may have questions. I answer a few of them in the following pages. I trust in the Holy Spirit to whisper the right answer to any questions crossing the mind of the reader of this story. It is good to notice questions from this story until the answer is found. The Bible should be enough for that. But if not, keep looking for an answer until you get connected to a good Christian friend or, better, a church leader who will be pleased to help you out. *Let us give some easy advice for anyone willing to live a forgiving life.*

5.1: How do you know that you have forgiven a person?

Let me speak from my experience. You know that you have forgiven a person or a group of people when you have peace in thinking about them. You can still feel the pain from their bad action but still wish them well and are able to do good to them whenever possible. Before you've really forgiven a person, often when you think about them, you may feel sad, mad or even sick.

A Christian life is to keep searching for true forgiveness, which is found only in Jesus Christ's death on the cross for all sinners. When we see our pain through his, we give him the lead over our feelings in life, we relax, and he takes over.

Remember that we serve a very patient loving God. He still loves our enemies and expects them to believe in Jesus and repent one day. According to the Bible, "The Lord is not slow in keeping his promise, as some understand slowness. Instead he is patient with you, not wanting anyone to perish, but everyone to come to repentance" (2 Peter 3:9). That truth is to always help us let God deal with our enemies. We cannot do much for people who hate us. The spirit leading them to do that rejects and runs away from the spirit in us. Only the spirit from hell can push a person to hate. We can only pray for these people. When their negative emotions keep stealing our peace, the best way I found is to avoid what brings out that hate toward us. If possible, we can also avoid them until their hate gets to the lowest or vanishes. The Bible tells us that "If it is possible, as far as it depends on you, live at peace with everyone" (Rom.12:18). The Holy Spirit speaking through Peter knows that it is sometimes hard or even impossible to live at peace with some people, especially those full of hate and jealousy or envy.

5.2: How do you keep forgiving people who hurt you? What is a practical attitude towards hurting feelings or hurting people?

There are so many books out there about this subject. As my previous pages showed, the Bible is the best.

The goal of this book is not to sell another expert way of forgiving. It is simply to share my story, hoping that hurt people can get some ideas about how to cope with the hurting people they meet in all situations of life. So many hurting people keep us distracted from our main goal in life while we are trying to recover from the hurt. To stay focused on our goal, we have to look at a *higher goal* than what the enemies are offering. The ultimate goal in all of us should be eternal joy with God the Creator. When we decide to look at him as our hero, our healer, and our comforter, hurting people will never have the last word over our destiny. When you decide that you want go to heaven one day and live eternity with God, if you really mean it, *nothing and no one will stop you other than yourself.*

5.3: Why is forgiveness a main topic in this book?

Speaking as a Christian pastor, my first quick response is that the same topic is one of the cornerstones of the Bible, which is the book used by God to judge the nations.

But personally speaking, as a sociologist, I believe that the relation between "cause and effect" is true in most of cases of what we do. I believe that "cause and effect" are two things that are always related or intertwined in our daily living. In other words, we as people, isolated or as a group, what we do can have explanation in terms of its origin, its cause and its good or bad consequences towards ourselves or others. This principle cannot always 100 percent be verified, because, as human beings, we cannot be all-knowing. But in general, knowing "why" gives a way to knowing "how". I will not go in details about this universal sociological principle. Keeping focus on the context of this book, a person has to know first of all *why* to keep forgiving in order to enjoy the benefit of it. That is the goal of my story.

I do not know about you, but I really want to keep my friendship with God. I want to be with him in heaven forever when I leave this life. I also know that unforgiveness is sin. That is why, for seven years in hurt, I wanted to see my prayers be answered about that. The Bible tells us that sin separates us from God. I have decided to willingly run away from anything bringing me to sin, whenever possible. For this book, we are talking about a specific sin. The sin of unforgiveness comes between at least two people. Because human kind is always looking for relationship, forgiveness always brings life into it. Therefore, forgiveness is a basic and unavoidable subject to address at all times for those who want to be with God forever.

5.4: How do you avoid unforgiveness settling in your soul?

We cannot avoid hurt. Bad people, mean people, and sad events are all over the place wherever we go. In these days of technology, they even invite themselves in through your computer or cellphone or answering machine and TV shows in your own residence. Our generation has to be strong enough in order to keep peace and joy in everyday life.

Because I cannot avoid mean people or sad events happening to me, I have learned to look at the person behind the bad thing happening. If it is a random bad event, I look to God and wait for him to comfort me and to make me strong and take me through safely. If there is a person or a group of people behind a sad circumstance happening to me, as long as I can handle it without getting hurt, I am okay with it. If I start to feel hurt then, I have to do something. If people involved are willing to change, things will be easy. It gets *tough with people who get willingly mean* to us. If I can, I tell them the risk of them being mean. I usually open up about it so we can talk about the issue right away. Later on, if they are not willing to agree on a solution or change, I tell them clearly that I move on and that I will keep only a very light relationship with them.

You have to be clear with people, especially when the truth can bring changes into a relationship. Nothing should stop you from praying for them. The Bible has enough instructions from God about not only the power of prayer, but also about what to change in order to bring the relationship back to true life. *I believe that a dead relationship is not worth living through. But I put my hope in Jesus, the only one who can raise the dead.* Great faith in God can bring life back.

Living in a dead relationship is bearable only in a sense of serving—that is, when you expect nothing in return. This way you cannot really get hurt. That is how true Christianity works: expecting reward only from God and God alone. If a Christian is that strong, he can go ahead out there and be willing to get hurt any time possible.

For those who sincerely cannot stand being in an ongoing hurting relationship, they have to talk about it and ask for help and understanding. If that is not enough, then it is better to avoid hurt instead of keeping hurts and unforgiveness inside of us. *It is poisoning to feel hurt and do nothing about it.*

For my dear Christian leaders, please remember: We have to always be ready to tell the reason of our faith, our deeds, our attitudes, and our choices. The Bible says, " But in your hearts **revere** Christ as Lord. Always be prepared to give an answer to everyone who asks you to give the reason for the hope that you have. But do this with gentleness and respect" (1 Peter 3:15). As long as there is a testimony about honouring God behind your choice, go for it.

We have not arrived home as long as we are still on earth. How do we stay in the right path with God leading us?

Knowing and choosing Jesus as our Saviour is the beginning of deliverance. Challenges remain in our way. We are not totally delivered yet here on earth. Our total deliverance is in heaven where, out of reach from the devil, eternal joy is reality. Only people eager to get there can handle the uncomfortable zone of life with the Bible and true church as their GPS.

5.5: What kind of troubles can we use as an excuse before God to keep sin inside of us?

My answer is clear: none. Human kind should starve to remain focussed on the path of God, no matter what kind of troubles are present. Our safe destination after death depends on this determination. Sin is always on our path but the more we discover God's love and His presence in all the places we go, the easier we get to see Him fighting for us against temptation. From this perspective, since only sin can disconnect us from God, we should avoid it and be quick to repent any time it happens. Knowing that nothing is unmovable in God's eyes is a great tool to allow Him into our daily relationships.

I have been serving Jesus Christ for forty years now. I have seen a lot in the Christian field. So many Christians assume that "they've arrived" just by the simple fact of saying the sinner's prayer for salvation. We, many times, neglect to walk the talk! I was that kind of person for seven years after the genocide in Rwanda. In my second dream, when the shooters got closer to me, I was showing off, to let them see how I do not have fear about being shot at or death itself. I even kept showing love and peace from God to the gunmen. Whatever good deeds I was accomplishing without total repentance were useless. My advice is to *never deceive ourselves* about having a good connection with God while keeping sin willingly in our life.

I paid the price for my lukewarm Christianity. Coming back to earth after my visions, I wish for no one to go to the hell I saw.

Here is my gold advice from my Christian journey: I found that the best way to never miss God's appointment is to keep doing good, serving him, keep doing his will, as much as you can, while waiting for him to intervene when troubles get in the way. It does not matter how long it takes. In doing God's will, we end up by meeting him because doing so keeps us in his path. Wherever his will is on earth, there he is. As it is in heaven.

5.6: Do you think God send angels to help us in life?

My answer is "yes". For example, we read in the Bible that "The angel of the Lord encamps around those who fear Him. And rescue them. (Ps. 34:7). It shows also that angels help those who will inherit salvation. (Heb. 1:14). Also, according to the vision I got, God can use real angels to help us stay in the right path.

God can also use "angels in person". Connecting with people who care about our relationship with God can save our life and stop us from running away from Him. A reconnection with my old friend Laetitia gave me hope that because she had forgiven and recovered joy of living, then I could make it, too. It was also encouraging to know that she was organizing prayers for me. Before that, I had friends, sure, but no one of them had promised to take me to God in prayer. I know that I really care for people and that I have so much love to give out. But I recognized that I needed emotional care like everybody else. That is what God came down to offer to me when I was left on my own. He not only used my friend's prayer group but also pushed heaven to open for me. He *sent angels to walk with me and to do the job on his behalf.*

After many mistakes, I learned a good lesson: If true Christians are to bring the Good News out to people, it is a mistake to expect comfort from people we serve. Some of them, not even having emotional feelings within them to begin with, cannot give any. No one can give what he does not have. Only God has all things we need in life. He has millions of ways to supply them to us.

After my visions in 2001 through 2013, Laetitia and I kept an on and off connection. Twelve years have passed by. When we seriously reconnected back in November 2013, we shared all about what was going on in our Christian walk. She could not ignore the pain I was facing from so long when many people had been blocking my path in serving God. I needed a big help again in order to keep going.

Laetitia invited me for a free vacation to her beautiful and peaceful home in Waterloo, Belgium. She even paid for my son, Jo-Victory's flight, to go and minister to some young people over there. We both needed that time of rest and care. Laetitia did it, even though she was so busy with her own family and with her pastoral care to her church in Charles Roy area. Connecting me to some churches helped me to preach the Gospel and to share my out-of-body testimony. Visiting five churches within a month gave me a great comfort and boosted Jo-Victory's calling as a young preacher. With such a good refreshment in Christ, my son and I came back home to Calgary, Canada, before Christmas in 2013. *God will never forget what Laetitia did for me. She has been used as one of many angels I have met in my life from time to time.*

5.7: How do you recognize people who can help you to stay in God's path?

The Bible is clear. Jesus told us that "we will know them by their fruits" (Mathew 7:15–20). Paul also gives some details about those fruits: "love, joy, peace, forbearance, kindness, goodness, faithfulness, gentleness and self-control" (Gal. 5:22–23). As I said before, we cannot give what we do not have.

True friends do not judge you. They wish you the best in life. They have right to criticize, correct, and, if you agree, build you up. We should not put too much trust into our own feelings or views. We should have trustworthy friends to whom we do not hide anything. For the best scenario, they should be challenging us in order to see us become the best we can be. I have been there and without trustworthy friends who knew better than me, I could never be an overcomer to this day.

My sorrow took root because I did not have a Christian friend to help me in the early troublesome moments of life, during and right after the genocide in Rwanda. Since I was out of Rwanda when God allowed the angels of death to take actions in the whole country, it was easy for people to think that I could not suffer that much. This was not the case, and God heard my cry and kept me alive until I met true friends again. Glory to Him forever and ever.

Do not get me wrong. I had friends all along those dark moments. Our church in Strasbourg, France, L'Église Evangelique La Bonne Nouvelle de Strasbourg- France, took care of my family very well when we were living there. I remember one of our best friends, the late Eugenie Brehem, visited us so often, tried to comfort us, but the wound was so deep that she could not really do much in comforting us during those hard moments. Other neighbours and friends from Rwanda did their best to show love to me but they could not reach deep in my soul. There is a corner of hurt inside of us that only God can heal. That is why I made him my friend forever.

5.8: Can we fool God?

No, we cannot fool God. He knows everything. When I was caught by a sudden death in both of my dreams, according to human sight and judgment, people who had seen me and heard how I talked could easily assume that if I died, I would go straight in heaven. My own feelings at that moment were telling me that everything was okay with me, that I was filled with the Holy Spirit and ready to go to heaven by the time I died. I was not aware of the impact of unforgivness over my destiny. But I saw the reality: We cannot fool God.

The Bible says: "You *cannot fool God*, so don't make a fool of yourself! You will harvest what you plant" (Gal. 6:7). God is the best judge. We better be true servants to him all the time, no matter what people say about us. Otherwise, see what can happen to a bad careless servant of God, according to Jesus himself: "The master of that servant will come on a day when he does not expect him and at an hour he is not aware of. He will cut him to pieces and assign him a place with the hypocrites, where there will be weeping and gnashing of teeth. (Matt. 24:50–51).

5.9: How can we remain focused on our journey to heaven all the time?

I am deeply convinced that there is a need for a 24/7 worship service for the souls of human kind.

I learned that a healthy brain keeps very long-term memory. So we have to choose what we stock in it from a very young age. Parents, kids, teachers, pastors—we all have to start working on this principle together from the early childhood.

During my second vision, *long-time memories played by themselves* while I was dying. Let me remind you what an old secular song did to me. I kept singing it until I missed my way to heaven. You can read details about this song in the first part of chapter 3.

Since I've seen so many times the fruits of a constant prayer and the danger of a careless Christian life, I always ask people if they are willing to join me in planting a kind of ministry that will help people to always be alert about sin, repent as soon as possible, and enjoy a renewed life with Jesus, hourly, daily, monthly, all year long. That kind of permanent 24/7 praise and prayer ministry is needed in as many corners of the earth as possible. People from all venues would greatly benefit from the ongoing intercession ministry. I know that there are some out here. But we need more prayer warriors especially these days when we see too many challenging situations all over the planet earth.

5.10: Are we, as human beings, permanent creatures?

My answer is clear: Yes we are. *Our real self does not die. It is hidden by God into our body system. Therefore, no one and nothing can kill us.* After we get Jesus's DNA by salvation, we get heavenly citizenship. Refusing Jesus's call brings people to hell for good. I read it in the Bible, and I saw it with my own eyes.

I agree with the Bible that life on earth is really a transition toward life in eternity. The self in all of us is made in the image of God; that is why it cannot die. That is also why we cannot have peace when our attitude and acts are contrary to that image. We are born with a permanent mark from heaven, a godly particle, which tells us the good and the bad. When we leave earth, we go to the good or to the bad side of the permanent spiritual realm, depending on our choices on earth.

According to my own experience from God, I can tell you that *after the last breath here on earth*, **no one else tells us**

that we are dead. We know it by the undying inner man of ourselves. It remains alert and very conscious of what is happening without the body.

During my second vision, for example, in September 2001, I knew that I was dead after the last deadly shot. *If you die now, you know that you know it.* Let me repeat it: *You know that you just died by the person inside of you. Your soul never dies and never leaves you. Nothing can kill it. It is that image of God in us that can never disappear.* It is our real self that we are supposed to keep safe and to help it meet God our Creator and live with him for Eternity in heaven. Such attitude brings constant peace in us.

Now, after the vision, I understand that not keeping our soul safe for God's use is exposing it for eternal torture and nonstop suffering with other bad souls in hell, as the Bible tells us. We better nourish our conscience with a good heavenly diet, the Bible.

Our conscience never dies and gets revived by God once we get out of our body.

As I've said before, the visions I had showed me how our body in flesh puts limitations on the ability of our soul and mind.

From my second out-of-body experience, when the killers were shooting my body without myself in it, I was able to look down on earth. I saw that the bullets shot toward my dead body were like foams of soap coming off the guns. I heard an explanation about that. A whispering voice was telling *my flying self*, in the air, that, once our soul is out of our body, it does not matter to God what happens to the dead body. Our body is there to help us to serve God in order to meet him once we die. I then understood once and for all that forgetting that truth makes us miserable, frustrated and even hopeless. We have to always remember that the fullness of joy in Christian doctrine comes from knowing about the resurrection and the glorification of our earthly bodies.

When my soul got out of my body, it was so easy to keep going up in the air, passing beyond the sky and crossing many levels in the heavens. After putting strong wings on my both sides, the angel of God was flying all along the way up there with me. The planet earth underneath us and other planets I saw in the air were so easy to catch, to see, and to somehow recognize what was going on within them. I understood that the senses in the spiritual realm are so powerful and clear. I cannot repeat enough how our earthly body puts a limit to our understanding of so many things happening in the spiritual realm around us. That is why the Bible is right in telling us to long for things from the Spirit of God (see 1 Cor. 2:14–16).

5.11: Do dead people lose their ability and conscience?

The Bible shows that we do not die really. Rather, we get transformed. "Behold, I tell you a mystery: we shall not all sleep, but we shall all be transformed" (1Cor. 15:51, Aramaic Bible in English).

According to the vision I got, not all earthly abilities of the dead get disabled.

I was frustrated and tortured by knowing that some of my abilities were reactivated after I died. From birth, God has put in me the gift of audacity and encouraging others, especially in hard times. I was spontaneously using those gifts at the time of my dreams. I wanted to come back to earth, at least once to tell people on earth how the Bible is so real. I badly wanted to invite people to take the Book of God seriously so they would not end up in the hell I saw. I wanted to ask the angel how to do that or to send him to earth, but I could not! *Knowing the right* thing to do but *not being able to do it! That was killing my soul* more than what the fire or the guns had done to my body.

5.12: Why should you read this book?

In the next pages, let me give you some of the benefit of taking time to read my story.

(a) No more fear of death.

I pray that people who will read this book will not fear death anymore but will get ready for it instead.

As I wrote about my two visions, I got to know a little bit more about the dying and dead people's feelings. That experience has helped me to care for dying people. When I get the chance to be with them, I make sure that their real self admits that they are sinners. If they are not yet born-again Christians, I then help them to repents from their sins and accept Jesus Christ as their saviour. Receiving forgiveness gives them a way to heaven immediately when their soul is separated from their flesh. If they are still alert and can remember to whom they did wrong, I help them to address the issue before their last breath. When it is not possible, we trust God for total forgiveness and eternal joyful life for the dying person. Knowing that death is only the beginning of another journey on the other side of life can help people to be smart enough in choosing the good side of the new journey. The choice starts here in what I call the Hopeland—beautiful planet earth. I really wish to pass on this message: None of us are alive by accident. Let us live as eternal beings for a happy future with God. What I saw made the Bible so real.

(b) The Great Commission makes more sense.

Those two visions boosted my faith and renewed my way of obeying the Great Commission given by Jesus Christ after his resurrection: "Then Jesus came to them and said, 'All authority in heaven and on earth has been given to me. Therefore go and make disciples of all nations, baptizing them in the name of the Father and of the Son and of the Holy Spirit, and teaching them to obey everything I have commanded you. And surely I am with you always, to the very end of the age'" (Matt. 28 18–20).

What I saw in my dreams helps me to willingly do good to people crossing my path daily. It's easier than before to encourage people to get saved and to always be quick in obeying God. All because of the powerful hand of God beyond the visible world we live in today.

(c) Life in hell or in heaven became more real.

When you have an afterlife experience and you come back to life, you know that heaven and hell are real. That is what it took for me to forgive people at any time possible. It is not easy but I do my best. That experience also helps me to tell other people about the risks of sin and the rewards of a victorious Christian life. The reality about God and heaven is so real—let us go for it.

Hell is also real and wide open for careless living people. Let us avoid it and help others to do the same. Disciple making is a matter of helping people to avoid life in hell. It is a revelation, a gift of knowledge, a permanent truth. True Christians are always busy, passing it on and on till Jesus comes back to bring us home. God loves that so much that he gets himself involved in it. What he needs is only our free will to agree with His.

(d) It takes the grace of God to do good without selfish interest. Knowing the truth does not necessarily make it happen.

The next day after my first vision of the underground miserable life, I began talking about that dream about hell, the angel, and so on. I kept asking my friends to pray for me so God could help me to obey him and forgive. I did not have energy to do so by myself. I kept telling God how I deserve to get mad and be angry with these bad people. Even though it became clear to me from the angelic show of the Bible that I had to forgive everybody quickly, it was not yet easy for me to obey. I understand today that only God can help us to do his will. Today, I understand better than before what Paul said in Roman 7:21: "I find then a law, that, when I would do good, evil is present with me." If only we could admit that truth and allow Jesus to lead our lives. That is the only way he can take charge of our lives. His leading breaks down our ego and removes the power of evil from within us every day. It is a progressive regenerating DNA of God in us through the Holy Spirit when we accept to follow Jesus' mission of saving people from death. His interests become ours, *not the other way around.*

This experience humbled me in some way. It was always easy for me to obey God before the genocide. My long-term sorrow made me more mature and more understanding and patient with people who struggle with any kind of sin. I learned that knowing the truth does not necessarily help us to do it right. It takes another effort of *free will* and personal determination. No one else will do that for us. It also takes a prayer life, a safe network with true friends and believers who are ready to help and to wait upon *God's timing* for his intervention. Ultimately, it takes the grace of God to go through all those steps.

(e) The hurting world needs Jesus.

As you can read in this book, the second vision helped me to forgive instantly. I do not need for the people who hurt me to apologize anymore before I forgive them. Jesus himself gave an order to hell not to hold me. I am so grateful to him. When you take him as a personal friend, he never leaves you nor forsakes you, and no power of hell can resist him. I love it! I was a hurting friend of God. He remembered me in my darkest moment of life on earth. I know for sure that he will keep watching over me until the end. He does the same for all who allow him to do his job.

One of the best attitudes to take in the hurting world we live in today is this: We have to get time to learn and grasp the meaning of the Love of God and the power of Jesus. It is the same power that raised him from the dead for us to live forever. It is the power of the Word from the mouth of God Himself, which makes everything come into being. Jesus is the "I AM", that power that we all need in order to live happy.

The enemy cannot hurt any friend of God before hurting God first. Since no power can do hurt to God, then we are out of reach from the hurting world, if we really hide ourselves in

Him. Roman 8:31 tells us this: "If God if for us, who can be against us". The answer is no one. We need great faith to walk in this truth of the Gospel in order to always be on the winning side of life.

People who are far from God cannot plan to do good without their own selfish ambitions. That is why they keep hurting anybody or anything found in their path, if that very thing does not make them happy. That is why people should get right with God first before getting right with others. Otherwise, they hurt.

It takes a revelation from God himself for a human being to be aware of the feelings of our loving God toward a sinner. That is why I believe deeply that the Gospel well preached, in words and deeds, is the best key for conflict resolution for people on earth at all times.

The Bible tells us how getting peace with God is possible. It is also free. It takes a willingness to recognize mistakes or bad thinking crossing the mind. Then by sincerely saying, "I am sorry, God, please help me to do right"; God loves and hears that prayer. Then He comes and helps. He has millions of ways of helping us out. He can speak straight to our mind. Because he is the one who sets up our mind, he is the best to speak to us and make himself understood. He can also use another person, a church member, a friend or some circumstances. He is omnipotent and omnipresent. He is the everlasting wisdom.

In the hurting world we live in today, even when you forgive people, some of them keep their guilt and stay away from you. Some people cannot forgive themselves, and because they do not learn from their mistakes, they keep running away from help and keep hurting more and more new people they cross on their path. The Church of Christ is supposed to be the best at addressing this issue. *Hurting or angry people* need to be understood. They *need help*, and the church should always be ready for them. Why the Church? Because a family of believers has power from the variety of gifts we get from God in order to care for one another. What I cannot do, someone else among believers can, and vice versa. The problem remains for people who run away from the Church. A lot of people try to join a church family and give up quickly. They should know that no church on planet earth is perfect yet. The cleansing power of the blood of Jesus keeps doing the job until He comes back to do things right.

Fortunately, among the hurt people, many are the ones who do not want to hurt back. That is why, by the grace of God, life goes on easily without recycling revenge. But I realized that some of those people choose to keep the hurt for themselves instead of dealing with it. I teach that only people who are aware of the hurt and ready to talk about it can enjoy the help if they express their need. Opening up about personal problems is a sign of humility. Humility also gives the key to God to work in our lives. That is why Scripture says, "God opposes the proud but shows favour to the humble" (James 4:6).

As I said, after the second vision, I decided to do more in helping as many people as I could to be able to forgive others. Since I was misunderstood and could not find help when I needed it for seven years, I can hear similar pain easily. It took a lot of grace from my Heavenly Father to do the job by himself. I do not take his mercy for granted. Today, I am ready to connect hurting people to God through the Bible, to pray for them and encourage those who are eager to help the hurting world around us. The emotional hurt is so real among us. Focusing on the unseen emotional hurt helps to gain peace of mind and then to be able to deal with the visible wounds and problems in the everyday life. Our communities need this approach in order to live out a happy life with our families, our neighbours, our cities, and ourselves. Even the governments get benefit from this. The truth is that it is almost impossible to lead unhappy people. And happy people are found in God's eyes. So let us respond to his calling and give glory to Him. He will do the same for us.

Before concluding, I am inviting people to read and cherish the Bible: it brings life. One of my favourite readings in the Bible is Luke, chapter 12. It has been a refreshing reminder of the cost of our obedience toward our heavenly Father. Reading and meditating on the Scripture is the best way to remain on the right path of the journey to eternal happiness with God in heaven.

Conclusion: Experiencing the judgement day made me more aware of time running out every day.

As you can read in my story, the sorrow of missing heaven motivated my zeal for Christ.

Later on, back to my body twice, I understood that the mind of a soul out of the body gets a clear and quick understanding of the mechanism of the spiritual realm. But at the same time, it loses its autonomy. It only gets to follow the rules of the after-life-world-masters.

These visions have helped me to use my freedom while I am still living in my body on earth. Once out of it, if I get a bad master to follow, I would be miserable for eternity. My two visions turned me to the King and Master Jesus Christ

for good. He is the master of my life forever. He cares for all
of us. Let's go meet him now. Now is the time! Forever and
ever. Amen.

The author shares her vision from God about life after death.

This book starts by describing the joyful life of the author until
the Rwandese genocide stole her peace for seven years. She
could not understand why and how she could forgive the ruth-
less people who turned her homeland into a bloody one, killing
a million of innocent people and destroying the meaning of
life for all genocide survivors and their Hutu friends.

Eugenie, being Rwandese herself, believes deep in her soul that
all Rwandese are related somehow. She never bought into the
ethnic classification that led to Hutus and Tutsis feeling different and many times, becoming enemies. Identity cards should
never push one ethnic group to feel they are worthy to live and
another to be killed. No one on planet earth has the right to
exterminate others. Be it for race, religion or any background,
all people are born naked, innocent and equal. Subdivisions
and subtitles should be done only for social accommodation
with goals of living in harmony for all. The majority of Hutu
people who have been always good by refusing to kill Tutsi and
choosing to hide some are the proof of that truth.

Being Christian from her young age did not really help her
when, in her late thirties, she saw her own people losing the
sense of life. Struggling to forgive brought a never-ending
sorrow into her soul. She was wondering how she could get
her joy back and keep preaching the Gospel in love for all.

She was bitter until God showed her, through two afterlife experiences, where the real bitter people go when they die. She visited hell twice: in June and then in September 2001. Each time, during a deep dream, she woke up desperate, thinking that she had died forever and that she was going to stay in hell with those bitter people forever.

Now that she got a second chance to be on planet earth, which she calls The Hopeland, she is using this opportunity to share her experience about the afterlife expedition she made. She saw angels in charge of leading dead people wherever they deserved to go. These angels appeared to her holding a big Bible that she was able to read and understand in full, within a very short time. The spiritual speed was at work in that. Her conscience, which resisted a consuming fire and many gunshots, never died. In both dreams, only her body died. The book gives details of her vision. It also goes into details about the meaning of eternal life in Heaven. The consequence of unforgiving souls is to live in a hopeless hell forever. For Eugenie, no one should go there, but life on earth is the only place to escape that sad ending of life, which never ends really for all of us. The joyful continuity of life is worth a try. For this, we shall do our best, and God does the rest.

Eugenie, hoping that you or someone else, by reading this book, can be able to forgive those who hurt you every day, decided to write this book. She has no doubt about the Bible judging all nations one day at the Judgment Day. She is begging all people to consider the truth of that Book that no one can escape from. According to her, there is no meaning of life out of the Bible. All meaning of life is found in it.

This is the summary of her advice for those willing to go to heaven: They have to be willing to forgive. Temptations are on the way for each one of us here on earth. So many mean, selfish, and angry people come into our lives every day. It is not fun. But the Holy Spirit is available to all of us. He is living in the hearts of true believers. He is our advocate, our counsellor, and our comforter. We have to join in and believe in Jesus in order to hear from him. Salvation is the key in this matter. Teaching about revenge is insanity. The Gospel does not do so. It clearly leaves that job to God who knows and sees all.

When we are hurt by other, we have to remember that forgiving is a command from God, not an accessory choice. Some people do not like to deal with personal issues. To forgive right away is not a magical procedure. It has to be a strict discipline. A person has to willingly work on it and get help from a pastor or from another Christian. The willing person has to aim for an ultimate *goal higher* than hurting back, and better than going to hell. An awareness of eternal life with God, or eternal condemnation, has to remain activated in our daily choices and activities until we die.

Hopeland: *Planet earth is our catching the hope playground. "There is no place like planet earth for human beings. Everything gets into being from heaven. We can make good or bad choice from all the things we cross on this given planet earth."*

I can get into more details when discussions are organized about this book in meetings, church services or conferences.

∞

Printed in Canada